BRAIN HACKS
FOR TRADERS

Harvey Walsh

shelfless

Brain Hacks For Traders
First Published 2015 by Shelfless
First Edition [P1.1]
ISBN 978-1518687204
Shelfless Ltd, Leigh-on-Sea, SS9 2AB, UK
WWW.SHELFLESS.CO.UK
Copyright © Harvey Walsh, 2015-2018

The right of Harvey Walsh to be identified as author of this work has been asserted in accordance with sections 77 and 78 of the Copyright, Designs and Patents Act, 1988.

You may not copy, store, distribute, transmit, reproduce or otherwise make available this publication (or any part of it) in any form, or by any means (electronic, digital, optical, mechanical, photocopying, recording or otherwise), without the prior written permission of the publisher. Any person who does any unauthorised act in relation to this publication may be liable to criminal prosecution and civil claims for damages.

LIMIT OF LIABILITY / DISCLAIMER OF WARRANTY: THE PUBLISHER AND THE AUTHOR MAKE NO REPRESENTATIONS OR WARRANTIES WITH RESPECT TO THE ACCURACY OR COMPLETENESS OF THE CONTENTS OF THIS WORK AND SPECIFICALLY DISCLAIM ALL WARRANTIES, INCLUDING WITHOUT LIMITATION WARRANTIES OF FITNESS FOR A PARTICULAR PURPOSE. NO WARRANTY MAY BE CREATED OR EXTENDED BY SALES OR PROMOTIONAL MATERIALS. THE ADVICE AND STRATEGIES CONTAINED HEREIN MAY NOT BE SUITABLE FOR EVERY SITUATION. THIS WORK IS SOLD WITH THE UNDERSTANDING THAT THE PUBLISHER IS NOT ENGAGED IN RENDERING LEGAL, ACCOUNTING, FINANCIAL, INVESTMENT, OR OTHER PROFESSIONAL SERVICES. IF PROFESSIONAL ASSISTANCE IS REQUIRED, THE SERVICES OF A COMPETENT PROFESSIONAL PERSON SHOULD BE SOUGHT. NEITHER THE PUBLISHER NOR THE AUTHOR SHALL BE LIABLE FOR DAMAGES ARISING HERE FROM. THE FACT THAT AN ORGANISATION OR WEBSITE IS REFERRED TO IN THIS WORK AS A CITATION OR POTENTIAL SOURCE OF FURTHER INFORMATION DOES NOT MEAN THAT THE AUTHOR OR PUBLISHER ENDORSES THE INFORMATION THAT THE ORGANISATION OR WEBSITE MAY PROVIDE OR RECOMMENDATIONS IT MAY MAKE. FURTHERMORE, READERS SHOULD BE AWARE THAT INTERNET WEBSITES LISTED IN THIS WORK MAY HAVE CHANGED OR DISAPPEARED BETWEEN WHEN THIS WORK WAS WRITTEN AND WHEN IT IS READ.

Cover Design by Shelfless. Keyboard image (modified) courtesy of JayWalsh at Wikimedia Commons, licensed under CC BY-SA 3.0

Risk Disclosure Statement

Day trading has large potential rewards, and also large potential risk. You must be aware of the risks and be willing to accept them in order to invest in the financial markets. Do not trade with money that you cannot afford to lose. The contents of this book is for general information purposes only. Although every attempt has been made to assure accuracy, we assume no responsibility for errors or omissions. Examples are provided for illustrative purposes and should not be construed as investment advice or strategy. Hypothetical or simulated performance results have certain inherent limitations; unlike an actual performance record, simulated results do not represent actual trading. Also, since the trades have not actually been executed, the results may have under or over compensated for the impact, if any, of certain market factors, such as lack of liquidity. Past performance is not indicative of future results.

Contents

INTRODUCTION	1
The Secret of Success	3
Trading Is Hard	7
Fear and Greed	11
Brain Hacking	13
Some Assumptions	15
Resources Page	17
THE HISTORY OF YOU	19
Introduction	21
The Hidden 90% of You	23
Your Personal War	27
Fear	35
Greed	37
Loss Aversion	39
COGNITIVE BIAS	43
Optimism Bias	45
Confirmation Bias	49
Illusory Correlation	55
Apophenia	65
Outcome Bias	75
Hyberbolic Discounting	77
Irrational Escalation	83
Heuristics	87
Contrast Bias	89
Social Proof	97
Scarcity	107
Ambiguity Effect	109

Anchoring	115
It's A Team Effort	123
LEARNED BEHAVIOUR	**125**
Introduction	127
Gambler's Fallacy	129
The Knowledge Gap	133
Over Trading	137
Attention!	143
MORE BRAIN HACKS	**155**
Hacking The Reward System	157
Magic Mentor	167
Meditation	173
NLP	182
Wrapping Up	185

INTRODUCTION

The Secret of Success

Imagine two traders. We'll call them Ashley and Casey, because then I don't have to decide if they're men or women. Ashley and Casey pick up a book on their favourite subject, read it, and learn a new strategy for day trading futures contracts.

Both of them have been trading for about a year. If someone persuaded them to take an IQ test, their results would be within a point of each other. They had a similar education, got about the same grades at school, and graduated with equivalent qualifications.

A day after reading the trading book, both of our heroes take to the market. They apply the strategy they have just acquired to the best of their ability.

They're trading the same contract, on the same days. They're looking for the same entry and exit signals, which means they should be buying and selling at the same times.

Ashley and Casey are clients of the same broker. They use the same software, running on identical computers, with internet connections that — by incredible coincidence — provide exactly the same speed and latency. Their charting software is the same, their orders are routed the same way, and they both experience identical slippage. Neither of them have any distractions in their trading environment, they're both in good health, and they both sleep well every night.

After a week of following the new strategy, they arrange to meet up to compare their results.

Ashley arrives early and downs a couple of drinks before Casey arrives.

Casey eventually turns up in a brand new car. "Sorry I'm late," Casey says. "Had to pick this baby up from the dealership. What do you think? Pretty cool, huh?"

Ashley is stunned. "How could you afford that?"

"With the money I made on the markets this week," replies Casey. "Best week ever! That new strategy is killer, don't you think?"

Ashley isn't sure if Casey is being serious. "Are you having a laugh? That strategy was a pile of tosh. I lost money every single day!"

Casey pulls out a broker statement and proves that great sums of money have indeed flowed inwards.

Thoroughly depressed, Ashley returns to the bar and orders something stronger.

Casey pays.

Okay, you get the idea. You might even have been there yourself. I know I have. It might be a book, or a new thread on a trading forum, a blogpost from someone I respect, or a video shared somewhere. The medium doesn't matter, it's the message.

A new strategy. A great idea. A surefire way to beat the market!

Except when I try it out, I don't get the results that were promised.

How can this be? Is the person who wrote the blog post or forum thread or video lying to me? Are they making up their results for a laugh? How can they succeed where I cannot? How can a strategy that works so well for Casey completely and utterly fail for Ashley? After all, they are as smart as each other, and they have equal opportunities to execute. Neither is at a disadvantage.

It's a question I used to ask myself daily, back when I started out trading. I think deep down I always knew the answer, but admitting it was hard. And therein lies the exact problem. The difficulty in seeing the difference between Ashley and Casey *is* the difference between them.

Seeing facts for how they truly are is at the heart of the issue.

Casey has no technical or environmental benefit over Ashley. But Casey does have one advantage. Casey has an ability to see the truth, and to act on it without hesitation. Casey has bridged the chasm between knowing what to do, and *actually doing it.*

In other words, Casey can execute.

If there is a secret of success in trading, it's this: *execution is everything.* The question then, is why is it that some traders can execute but others can't? By the end of this book, you'll know the answer to that question.

Trading Is Hard

Trading is one of the toughest professions I know of. It is also one of the easiest. How can both of those statements be true? Anyone who has already tried trading probably knows the answer intuitively.

Trading is easy in the same way that giving up smoking is easy. You just stop smoking.

Trading is easy in the same way that losing weight is easy. You just eat less and exercise more.

Trading is easy in the same way that winning a Formula One Grand Prix is easy. You just drive faster than everyone else on the grid.

Trading is easy in the same way that learning another language is easy. You just memorise a lot of words, grammatical rules, and exceptions.

Trading is easy in the same way that building a skyscraper is easy… You see where I'm going with this, right?

All of these activities are easy, but they are also incredibly tough, and only a tiny minority of people succeed. In the case of Formula One racing, only one person can win any given race. At least with trading, everyone *can* be a winner (yes, really).

The problem, of course, is one of mental fortitude. It's what I call *head stuff*. Knowing what to do and actually doing it are not the same thing.

Execution is everything.

If you're trying to lose weight, you know that eating the big cream doughnut is wrong, and that eating an apple instead is the better choice. That's easy. Everyone knows that. Choosing the apple over the sticky, sweet doughnut when both are sitting in front of you on the counter? That's tough. The little voice in your head says *'Go on, just this once. Look at all that creamy goodness. Imagine how delicious that will be! The apple will still be there tomorrow. Have the doughnut!'* Then another little voice says *'That doughnut is a really bad idea. Think how many calories are in it. You'll have to run three miles to work those off. The apple is really nice too. Just have the apple.'*

Which voice do you listen to? The battle rages, arguments and counter-arguments fly back and forth. You make your choice, and then you live with the consequences.

Sometimes it's the right choice, sometimes the wrong one. Either way, you've only won or lost a battle, never the war. There are always more choices to make.

I may be over-dramatising a little. Perhaps not everyone has such a verbose inner monologue. But everyone does struggle with doing the right thing, with deciding between conflicting thoughts. It's these decisions, these tiny split-second moments in which a choice is made, that make or break our dreams. And unfortunately for us, human beings are not very good at making good choices.

But we can get better.

That's what this book is ultimately about. Getting better at doing the right thing, at making good choices.

I've been teaching trading for well over a decade, and have been trading for longer still. I've worked with traders and would-be traders at every level, from absolute beginners right through to hedge fund managers with millions, sometimes billions of dollars in play. Every single one of them, myself included, struggles with the same problems at some time or another. The successful traders just manage those problems better. They make the right decision more often than the wrong one.

Fear and Greed

I have yet to meet a trader who has not experienced some form of fear or greed when trading, and I've met a lot of traders. These apparently destructive emotions are nothing to be ashamed of. Indeed they exist for very good evolutionary reasons. Unfortunately when it comes to entering and exiting trades, they are our number one enemy. Who has never been afraid to enter a big trade for fear of taking a huge loss? Who hasn't held on to a position just a bit too long, greedy for more profit? And who can honestly say they have always exited a losing trade at the earliest opportunity, and have never waited just another few seconds to see if it will turn around? We've all done it, and it's one of the most common reasons that traders fail to realise the profits that they are truly capable of.

Most trading books will tell you that you must learn to banish fear and greed, and leave it at that. They're not wrong, but the advice is as useful as saying that to give up smoking you must learn to stop putting cigarettes in your mouth. If only it were that simple.

If we are to banish fear and greed from our trading, we first have to understand what those emotions are, where they come from, and what it is they are trying to achieve. After all, they didn't just pop into existence for the fun of it. They are there for a reason, and a very good reason, too.

Actually, I think we can do better than just conquering our fear and greed. I believe that when we understand them properly we can subvert them, turning their awesome power a hundred and eighty degrees, and have them work *for* us, rather than against us.

Brain Hacking

Before we get into the meat of the subject, it's probably a good idea to explain what brain hacking is. My dictionary provides a couple of definitions for the word *hack*:

Verb: Gain unauthorised access to data in a system or computer.

Verb: Program quickly and roughly.

Noun: A piece of computer code providing a quick or inelegant solution to a particular problem.

Okay, so I'm using a little artistic licence in my appropriation of the term. I'm not suggesting you gain unauthorised access to your own brain. (Is that even possible?) And I'm certainly not suggesting that we come up with any inelegant or rough solutions to the problem of execution in trading.

What I am suggesting is that you can *access a system* (your brain) to implant *quick solutions* to the *particular problem* of trade execution.

If you've ever seen the movie Wargames, you'll have an idea of what I mean. In the film, Matthew Broderick's character, David, hacks into the US Missile Defence System and inadvertently sets off a chain of events that could ultimately lead to the launching of nuclear missiles against Russia. World War Three will ensue, and mutually assured destruction will follow. It's end-of-the-world stuff.

To save the planet, David hacks into the system again and subverts it, turning it against itself, forcing it to learn that war is not the answer. It's all a bit far-fetched, but the theory is basically the same as what I'm aiming to do with this book.

Your brain is, for reasons we'll discover shortly, trying to sabotage your trade execution. By *hacking in* and subverting its programming, you can use its power to enhance your trading performance instead of hindering it. Like the judo black belt who uses his opponent's own strength against him, you can use your brain's considerable strength to overcome its tendency to prevent you from executing your trades correctly. You won't save the world from a nuclear strike, but you should find you make a lot more money from the markets.

Some Assumptions

This book is suitable for traders working in any time frame, be it scalping, day trading, swing trading, or longer term strategies. The methods we will cover also work equally well regardless of what it is that you trade. It doesn't matter if your preferred market is the NASDAQ, the LSE, or any other stock exchange. It makes no difference if you trade stocks or futures, forex, commodities, precious metals, oil…anything at all. Whatever the instrument and time frame, traders face the same challenges beyond their trading strategy. Knowing what to do is one thing. Having the mental discipline to do it is quite another.

This book is all about the discipline part. It's about having the mental fortitude to take a loss without hesitation; to ignore the nagging doubts that plague us all from time to time and enter trades fearlessly; to keep going when the chips are down, when it feels like the market is against you. It's about that head stuff, and it's what really separates winners from losers in this game.

Because we're dealing with discipline and not the mechanics of trading, I must make some assumptions about you, the reader:

You already have a trading strategy, which is to say, you know what to trade and how to trade it. You're not blindly buying and selling randomly, hoping to turn a profit.

Your strategy is proven to have positive expectancy. Either you or someone you trust has back or forward tested it, so you know that provided you follow your strategy, you will make money.

You have a good understanding of the basics, and are familiar with common trading terms. You know the difference between going long and short, you know what market, limit, and stop orders are.

If the above doesn't make any sense to you, or if you're just starting out on your trading adventure, then you should probably put this book to one side and go and learn the basics. Come back to it once you've got your strategy worked out, you'll get more out of it that way. And if you're looking for a book to get you up to speed quickly, then might I humbly recommend you have a look at mine — you'll find the details at the end of this book.

Resources Page

Throughout this book I will make mention of certain software, apps, websites, and other useful tools. Rather than provide links directly in the text only to have those sites move, or apps disappear a week after publication, I have put together a *Resources Page* on my website. Keeping the links online means I can update them when anything changes, or add to them if new and useful sites and services come to my attention.

You can find the Resources Page at:

    www.daytradingfreedom.com/brain-hack-resources

THE HISTORY OF YOU

Introduction

I hated history at school. "It's a thing of the past!" I used to say to my teachers, thinking I was being smart. Turns out, history's pretty important. If we want to know the future, or even to understand the present, a good way to start is by studying the past.

If we want to get to the bottom of what drives us as traders to make bad decisions, then we need to know something of our past. Where does our fear and greed come from? What are these apparently destructive emotions and behaviours trying to do? A trip into our history can answer these questions. When we understand the reasons we do what we do, we can take informed action that will move us from being a slave to our fear, to using it as a source of power.

To get some answers, I have a special tool up my sleeve. Literally. See? It's here, strapped to my arm. I have one for you to. Here, stick this on your wrist. Don't worry about the flashing lights, that just means it's working. I call these things vortex manipulators (yeah, I stole the name). They're going to let us travel in time. We're going backwards. Not far, in the grand scheme of things. The universe is thirteen point eight billion years old. We're only going back fifty thousand years or so. I've pre-programmed your vortex manipulator so all you have to do is tap that button…there! That's it, journey's over. Time (sorry!) to have a look around.

Excellent, we've arrived exactly where and when I had hoped. We've set down just outside a village. I say village, but that's perhaps too recent a term for this place where early modern humans have chosen to live.

You see the beardy fellow over there? That's Bob. Bob is a homo sapien, one of the first. His recent ancestors were Neanderthals, and Bob is on the cusp of an evolutionary shift.

I know what you're thinking: "Harvey, you've lost the plot." Maybe, but Bob's a pretty important guy. Watching Bob can teach us all sorts of things about ourselves, because we're all Bob's descendants. Bob lives on in me, you, and everyone else alive today.

We'll be checking in on Bob later on, but before that we need to know a little more about how our brains work so we can effectively hack them.

The Hidden 90% of You

Would you say that you are in control of your actions? That your decisions are well thought out and are based on logic and reason? Or do you sleepwalk through life, operating on auto-pilot, daydreaming about dinner, or what you're going to watch on television later?

I suspect most people will answer that they are in control. It's what we want to believe about ourselves.

In a manner of speaking, every one of us is in control of our lives. We all have a brain, and that brain dictates our actions. Is that what we mean by control though? Is a drug addict, so desperate for their next fix that they are pushed to mug an innocent person and steal their wallet, in control of their actions? What about someone who has been put into a trance by a stage hypnotist? When they bark like a dog, or tuck into an onion as if it was a delicious apple, are they in control?

In both these cases, the subject is in control of their actions in so much as it is the electrical activity of the neurones in their brains that is causing their behaviour. Yet I suspect in both cases, most of us would say that no, the subjects aren't truly in control, because they are not really aware of their actions on a conscious level.

And that brings us back to my original question — are you in control of *your* actions?

Here's the reason I ask: according to research, up to 90% of what happens in our brains happens on a subconscious level. Ninety percent of all our thinking, decision making, and action, happens without us being aware of it. Like the hypnotised stage subject, or the crazed drug addict, the vast majority of what goes on inside our heads is *outside* of our direct control!

If that's a scary thought, don't worry. The word *direct* was a very important part of that sentence. As we'll see going forwards, there are still ways of accessing the hidden 90%, and brain hacking is all about doing just that.

Our brains work a bit like our computers. On a PC or a smartphone, what happens on the screen is just a tiny proportion of everything that's going on inside. Let's take the phone as an example. You might be reading your Facebook timeline, but the device is doing an awful lot more than just showing you what your friends had for lunch. Somewhere in the background it's communicating with a cell tower, letting it know where you are should someone try and call you. It might be downloading some updates to its operating system. A subroutine somewhere will be doing housekeeping work, clearing up space that was being used by the last app you had open and making it available for the next one. More subroutines will be monitoring the battery, charging it if the phone is plugged in, and trying to find ways to discharge it as slowly as possible if not. A clock is ticking, even if none is shown on the screen. It's checking every second to see if you've set an alarm and if so, if that alarm is due to sound. Your personal assistant — Siri, or Cortana, or whatever — is listening out in case you ask it something. The list goes on and on. There are literally hundreds of tasks happening that you cannot see.

Your brain is exactly the same. A lot of its work goes unnoticed. Some of its hidden lower level functions are obvious. It's sending electrical signals to your heart, making it beat regularly. It's inflating and deflating your lungs so you breathe. It's taking in data from your nerves, working out if you are hot, cold, in pain, hungry, or tired. It's moving your muscles, holding you upright, and making you turn the pages of this book. You don't actively think about any of these things, they just happen.

There's a whole lot more that just happens too, and some of it is quite surprising.

Deciding whether we like something or someone is controlled subconsciously. Any emotional decision happens without conscious thought. We don't think, *'Right, for the next twelve minutes I'm going to be happy.'* Joy, sadness, fear, greed, apprehension, these are all things that we might say happen *to* us, but in truth they are the result of activity within our brains. We take in information, our neurones fire accordingly, and the results are felt as emotion.

And still we can move up into even higher level functions. Many of the decisions that we think are within our direct control really aren't. Most buying decisions, for example, happen within our subconscious mind. When we decide to make a purchase, the impulse is emotional. We want the item. The conscious mind only comes into play later, when we try and justify the decision to ourselves. We can be as analytical as we want, and we might like to think we're making an informed decision when we hand over the cash for something, but actually that decision was made long ago, before we were even aware of it. Marketing people know this well, which is why the most effective advertisements tug at our heart strings or play on our fears.

When we talk, most of what we say comes out without thought or effort. It's no coincidence that 90% of sentences spoken are not unique. We're running on auto-pilot, churning out canned responses.

There's a reason for all this background processing going on in our heads. The world is complex, and we are complex machines within it. If we had to actively think consciously about every piece of information we encounter, about how to move our mouths to form the words we want to say, about how fast to make our hearts beat to keep up with the physical needs of our bodies at any given instant, we'd probably explode. There's just too much going on. So our subconscious acts like our personal assistant, taking that load off our shoulders and handling anything that doesn't really need our input.

Like any good assistant, our subconscious works as a filter. Any information that our senses take in passes through it. It gets to decide what's useful and what's not. Anything it can deal with, it will. And of the stuff it can't deal with directly, the rest will either be passed on to the conscious mind for consideration, or — more likely — dumped. Dumping information is an effective way to save time and energy.

It's a good system, but it's not perfect. Trouble can arise because, like many personal assistants, our subconscious sometimes has ideas above its station. It can get carried away and take on too much, filter out too much, discard too much. We've become so reliant on it, we don't notice when it's hindering rather than helping. It uses rules and procedures that are, for the most part, highly efficient. But when we do something out of the ordinary, those same rules can tangle us up and get in the way. Our subconscious minds, 90% of our brain's activity, are not always operating to the same priorities as our conscious minds. And that can lead to cerebral conflict and poor decision making. We're simply not as in control as we think we are.

Your Personal War

You are at war. You might not know it, but there is a fight raging inside your head right now. It's a civil conflict between different regions of your brain, and it's been going on since before you learned to think for yourself.

Part of your brain is telling you to keep reading this book, because it's going to teach you how to be a more profitable trader, and that means you'll have more money and all the benefits that go along with it. I heartily support this argument, by the way.

But another area of your brain is competing with this message. It's telling you to get up and go and procreate, or acquire some food supplies, either by hunting or — more likely, I'll admit — shopping. It might be urging you to eat something. It could even be suggesting you go out and kill or harm some enemies that might be threatening your superiority.

As if that wasn't enough, there's another zone of your grey matter that's fighting its corner. It's the lazy part. It's probably suggesting you switch on the telly and watch a film, or listen to some music, or play a video game, or go to sleep. Anything that will let it shut down and avoid working.

These kinds of conflicting thoughts are ever-present. Sometimes we can block them out easily enough, other times, not so much.

As in any war, each side thinks it is fighting the cause of righteousness. In this case at least, each side is quite correct.

The bit that wants you to keep reading? It's thinking about your financial security. A noble aim. The bit that wants you to go shopping or hunting? Obviously it's thinking about filling your belly to provide you with the energy to stay alive. Can't argue with that.

What about that nagging voice suggesting you go and make babies? It's thinking longer term. All the food in the world won't keep you alive indefinitely. Sooner or later you're going to need to produce some offspring to keep your genes in the pool. Perfectly reasonable.

And the bit that wants you to put on a DVD? Well, that's a bit more selfish. That's your brain trying to conserve energy by avoiding any kind of work at all. Thinking is very expensive in terms of energy consumption. Your brain accounts for just 2% of your body weight, yet it consumes up to 25% of the glucose and 20% of the oxygen in your bloodstream. When you are actively thinking about something, your brain is burning about 1.5 calories a minute. To put that into context, walking uses up about 4 calories a minute. But when your brain switches off thinking mode and idles, its consumption tanks, and it burns up just a tenth of a calorie per minute. So if it can convince you to remain inert and allow it to shut down, it will make major energy economies, which in turn means less need to go out hunting (or shopping), and that means less chance of you being killed by a lion. Or run over by a bus. Either way, it's improving your chances of still being here tomorrow.

These needs that your brain is trying to fulfil are all very basic. They're all concerned with making sure that you, or a direct derivative of you, continue to walk the Earth. Any time you decide to do something that conflicts with these basic survival needs, your brain is going to fight you.

Unfortunately it gets worse. These *physiological* requirements are just one layer of a multi-layer hierarchy of needs, and your brain has been programmed by thousands of years of evolution to try and meet all of them.

Back in 1943, American psychologist Abraham Maslow published a paper in which he described this hierarchy of needs. Though Maslow himself never portrayed it this way, the hierarchy is often illustrated as a pyramid, with the most fundamental needs forming the solid base. Each level up on the pyramid represents needs or motivations of lessening importance.

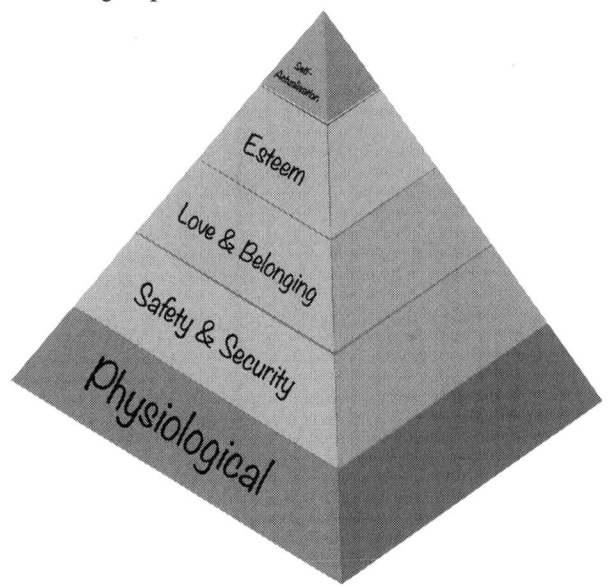

Although Maslow's work has been criticised over the years, there's little argument that most human beings are subject to all of these needs. The order might change for different cultures or different individuals, but the point is that any decision we ever make — whether it be what to have for dinner, whether to take a trade, or where to buy a house — is influenced to some degree by every layer of the pyramid. Let's look at those layers so that we can better understand what we're up against when we make decisions about our trades.

Physiological

I've already covered most of these above. Physiological needs are those that are physically necessary for life to continue. We need to breathe, drink, and eat, roughly in that order. Any prepper will tell you about the rule of three: broadly speaking, the human body cannot survive without air for three minutes, water for three days, and food for three weeks.

As a trader you might think that none of these physiological needs come into play when you are buying and selling your stocks or futures or currencies. That's true on the face of it; as long as you are fed and watered, your brain isn't going to spend too much effort pulling you away from the screen in order to get more sustenance down your throat. However, our old friend evolution means that it's a bit more complicated than that.

For thousands of years we had to take care of our physiological needs individually. When Bob the early human was hungry, he had to go out and forage or hunt. Bob developed a very particular set of skills, as Liam Neeson might say, and although those skills might be long forgotten to modern human beings, the instincts they fostered live on in the darker recesses of our brains. As we'll see, those instincts can and will come back and bite us when we least expect it, and they absolutely affect every single trade we make. Fortunately, as well as being traders, we are brain hackers. We can hack our instincts and use them for good rather than evil.

SAFETY & SECURITY

With food in his belly and air in his lungs, Bob's next priority was to stay safe. There's no point being fattened up if that's just going to make him the perfect meal for a neighbourhood tiger. Bob needs some physical security, somewhere safe to live. That means a cave with a roaring fire protecting the entrance.

Back in the present, most of us have done away with caves, preferring houses or apartments. But unlike Bob's home, our shelters come with strings attached. Bills, mostly. Heating, power, water, internet — all the essentials of life must be paid for. That means we need money, or financial security.

Naturally, we spend a lot of time obsessing over this level of the hierarchy. Modern life is expensive. To meet most of our safety needs we have to spend. Doctors to look after our fragile bodies, tradesmen to keep our accommodation in good condition, healthy food, insurance plans in case things go wrong, suitable transport to move us about without getting killed, the list goes on.

As traders we are financially independent, by which I mean we don't turn up to work every day and expect a pay cheque at the end of the month. Our payday depends entirely on our performance. If we screw up, we are quite literally putting our own safety at risk. Failure to make a profit every month means bills won't get paid, insurance will lapse, and our shelter won't be maintained. Take it to the extreme and we'll have to start worrying about our physiological needs too. It's no wonder we obsess over this layer of the hierarchy more than most.

Love & Belonging

Maslow suggested that human beings are essentially pack animals. We need to feel we are part of a social group. That could be a small group, like a family, a larger group, like a company or organisation, or even a transient group, like fans of the same sports team. If we are kept in isolation, we feel incomplete, as though some part of us is missing.

The need for love and belonging can be so strong it can sometimes override the lower level of safety. How many people remain in abusive relationships because they fear being alone more than the violence they suffer at home?

Unless you are trading in a bank or institution, you probably work alone. Trading isn't a group activity. It requires focus, attention, and concentration. Our decisions are ours and ours alone. That can be a great and freeing feeling, but our need for belonging is always there in the background. It's what tempts us to join internet forums and chatrooms. We're desperate to discuss our performance and ideas with our peers.

There's nothing wrong with that when it's done outside of market hours (provided we don't become distracted by shiny new ideas that lead us away from our own path), but problems often arise when traders join real-time chat rooms. They demand attention, leaching off concentration and brain power until we're spending more time talking than watching the chart. Trader beware!

Esteem

Being in a group is great, but once accepted, we need more. We need to feel *respected*. We crave the recognition of others. However much we might like to think we don't care what people think of us, deep down we're all obsessed.

Any cursory glance through the society pages of the newspapers or the gossip magazines will demonstrate that.

We attach levels of status to everyone; not just celebrities, but friends, family, even strangers. When we meet someone new, we're subconsciously sizing them up from the moment we lay eyes on them, judging them and pigeon-holing them in a social hierarchy.

Even before we get to worry about keeping up with the Joneses though, we have to meet our own expectations of ourselves. Nobody wants to feel worthless, useless, or pointless. We are our own harshest critics, constantly evaluating our place in the world.

Esteem can be a tricky problem for traders. Losing trades are an inevitable part of our business. They are to be expected, and depending on strategy, may even make up the majority of all the trades we take. But taking a loss means taking a direct hit on our self-esteem. Our tendency is to think that we got something wrong, that we made a mistake somewhere along the line. Weathering the constant battering of loss is tough for even the most hardened among us.

Self-Actualisation

As we arrive at the peak of Maslow's pyramid, we find self-actualisation. We seek to ascend to become the very best person we can be, fulfilling every ounce of our potential. What that means in real terms will be different for everyone. It may be that for one person, achieving self-actualisation will require them to change the world in some way. Steve Jobs famously wanted to make a dent in the universe. For another, raising a family is the very pinnacle of their ambition.

It's unlikely that trading in and of itself is the ultimate aspirational goal of many, but the summit of the pyramid still exerts pressure on our trades because in order to reach it, each and every layer below must be fulfilled.

Gravity Wins

As hard as we work to scale it, the pyramid of needs is always trying to drag us down to the basement. We may well want to reach the higher levels, but our subconscious — the 90% of what's going on in our head — is more concerned with keeping the foundations solid. Even if we should manage to ascend to the lofty heights of self-actualisation, we face an ongoing battle to stay there.

Now we know what are brains are trying to do for us, let's look again at our old enemies fear and greed.

Fear

Fear is our number one driver for survival. It is a primal emotion that resides deep in the amygdala — the oldest part of the brain, and one that we have inherited from our ancestors like Bob and the species which came before him.

Long before human beings developed the brain capacity to think logically and strategically, our basic fear response kept us alive. It made sure Bob ran away from predators. It drove him to find shelter, and it made him protect his offspring.

Fear is so successful at ensuring the continued existence of life that it has survived every step of evolution.

In our current form as an intelligent and dominant species, we no longer need to worry about having our lunch pinched by a bear, or about becoming a tasty snack for a tiger. The tables have turned; we're the predators now. And yet even though we have developed huge, complex brains that are capable of incredible feats of logic and imagination, fear is still so deeply entrenched in our heads that we can have enormous difficulty overcoming it, even for seemingly simple tasks. Just witness the number of phobias that afflict people from all walks of life. Intelligent people who are perfectly able to rationalise flying as statistically the safest form of transport can be paralysed by fear. They're unable to step aboard an aircraft, but they'll happily drive to the airport in a car, a means of transport that is a staggering three hundred and twenty-five times more likely to kill them than the aeroplane (data based on US transport statistics for 2005).

A fear of the dark can keep adults and children awake all night when they know full well that there is absolutely nothing threatening lurking in the shadows.

My brother-in-law even has a crippling fear of vegetables! He knows that they can't hurt him, that eating them will provide him with vitamins and minerals which will improve his health, and he knows they are tasty. But because he once choked on a carrot when he was a lad, his fear response overrides all logical thinking and prevents him from popping so much as a pea into his mouth.

Our fear response is so deeply embedded within us that we can never hope to eliminate it. Instead we must learn to control it. Or better yet, use it.

Greed

Almost all the other problems we encounter in our trading are born of fear. Even greed is a response to that emotion.

Greed is another survival instinct that can be traced back through our evolution. Being afraid of predators kept Bob from being killed, but not being eaten is not enough to stay alive. Bob also had to eat. The trouble is, so did the other early humans. The more they ate, the less there was for Bob. Evolution says the fittest will survive. If Bob was to stick around, then it was in his interests to take more than his fair share. More food for Bob meant less for his competitors, which in turn meant he would grow stronger and they would grow weaker. To paraphrase Gordon Gekko, greed is good.

In modern society there should be more than enough to go around. There's really no reason to take more than we need. But again, the greed response is etched into our amygdalae, and no matter how equitable we may like to think we are, we are all greedy hoarders deep down.

Fear is the engine that drives our subconscious. To serve its needs, human beings have developed a number of higher level behaviours that whirr away in the background, informing our choices and nudging our decisions in a certain direction. Most of the time we're blissfully unaware of them. We may not even realise they exist at all.

These behaviours are called *cognitive biases*.

We can't switch off our fear engine (and nor should we), but we can absolutely subvert it via these higher level biases. We can hack them and have them help us, but first we need to know what they are, and what it is they're trying to do.

Loss Aversion

If fear is the engine of our subconscious, then loss aversion is the satnav. We don't want to lose our lives, and that means not losing our health, food, shelter, and all the other needs at the bottom end of Maslow's hierarchy. Obtaining these things is hard and takes energy. Keeping them is easier than having to reacquire them. Loss aversion steers our actions, calling on the power of our fear to protect our assets.

There's little doubt that human beings wouldn't be here to worry about trading performance if Bob and his friends hadn't evolved loss aversion. But loss aversion can play havoc with our trading performance. It discourages us from taking the risks that are inherent in our business. It whispers to our all-powerful subconscious, *'Don't put your money on the line, you might lose it!'* We let the trade pass us by, then regret it because we discover that it was by missing the trade that we actually ended up losing money — the profit we would have made!

Here's where it gets really tricky. Miss out on enough profits through missed opportunities, and loss aversion does an about turn. Like the satnav calculating a new route when the road ahead is blocked, it figures out that we're losing too much profit by not taking risks. It recalibrates in real time and whispers a new message to our suggestible subconscious: *'Take this trade! It doesn't matter if it's not quite right, we can't risk losing out on the profit.'*

We don't stand a chance. Or do we?

Actually, I think we do. Let's draw another pyramid, like Maslow's hierarchy:

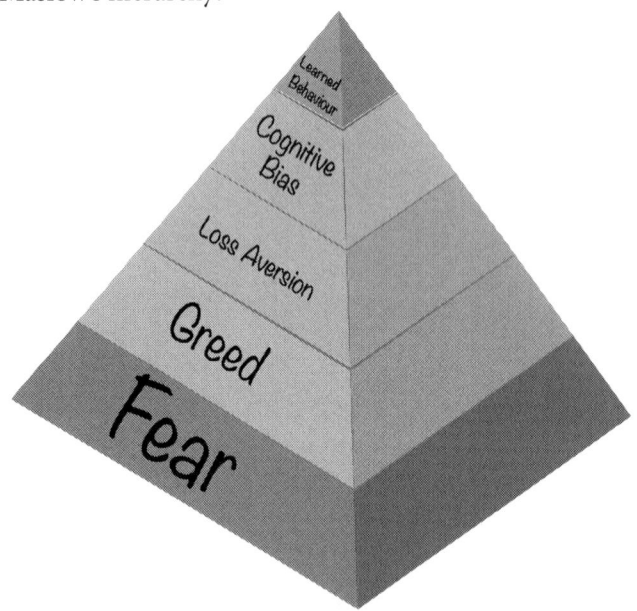

Pyramid with layers from bottom to top: Fear, Greed, Loss Aversion, Cognitive Bias, Learned Behaviour

I'm calling this *Walsh's Hierarchy of Action Motivators* because it means I get to use the handy acronym W.H.A.M.!

The layers of this pyramid represent the levels of our subconscious mind which motivate our decision making process, and therefore our actions. They present challenges that we must overcome if we are to take full control of our trade execution. Each layer builds on the others below. The higher up the pyramid we go, the easier it is to hack these *Motivators*.

We've already looked at fear, greed, and loss aversion. Those are the most difficult layers to change. Instead of trying, we can make our lives much simpler by subverting the upper two levels. That way we still get to use the lower level power, but we deploy it in a direction that better serves our needs. If that sounds greedy, it is. See? We're already hacking WHAM!

Let's dive in deep to level four, the cognitive biases.

V

COGNITIVE BIAS

Optimism Bias

I'm confident. You're confident. Everyone is confident. Even the most pessimistic person you know is confident — on a subconscious level. We have to be, because if we were realistic about the enormous challenges the world throws at us, we'd give up, curl up, and die. Whether it be war, climate change, economic meltdown, crime rates, house prices, or the idea of the eventual heat death of the universe, if we choose to look, there is always something we could be worrying about. The sheer number of insurmountable problems in the world means that individually we could never hope to overcome them all. If we spent our lives dwelling on all of them, we'd never get anything done.

So we don't think about them. We filter the input from our senses. We have an inbuilt *optimism bias* that works like the spam folder in our email, intercepting information that we don't want to know about, or that doesn't match our world view, and discarding it before it ever reaches our conscious mind.

There's a well-known experiment that demonstrates this bias nicely. In the experiment, a test subject is asked to rate the chances of a series of things happening to them. For example, they might be asked, "How likely do you think it is that you will contract cancer in your lifetime?" The subject responds with a percentage; perhaps they think they have a 10% chance. Then they're given the actual answer based on statistical data. In the case of getting cancer, the chance is actually 30%. They're asked the next question, and the process goes on.

So far so simple. Here's where it gets interesting. Once the subject has answered all of the questions, they then go through the whole set a second time. This time round they know all the correct answers. When the question about cancer comes up, they should answer 30%, because five minutes ago they were told that this is the actual statistical risk of them contracting the disease. And yet in almost every case, if the subject had previously underestimated the risk, they give the same answer they gave before. But if they had overestimated the answer the first time round, for example, if they thought their risk of cancer was 50%, then the second time they are asked the question they modify their response and give the actual, lower, figure.

The experiment demonstrates the tendency for people to accept positive information — that which is deemed beneficial — and to reject negative information. There is no shortage of other studies which demonstrate the same phenomenon. For example, surveys show that newlyweds consistently predict their marriages will last their lifetime, even when they are shown divorce statistics which imply that's unlikely to happen. University graduates underestimate the time it will take them to get a job and overestimate their likely starting salary. Even the pessimists among us are, deep down, irrationally optimistic.

For us as traders, optimism bias presents an obvious problem. We rely on charts and data to base our trading decisions on. We have to interpret raw information. But if our subconscious mind is filtering out anything that doesn't match what we *want* to see, if it's rejecting bad news, then we're not getting the full picture. We're making choices based on partial facts.

Our built-in optimism means we have a tendency to see what we'd like to see, rather than what's really there. When we're in a trade that's not going according to plan, we'll neglect the signals on the chart that are telling us it's time to exit, and instead focus on anything, no matter how small, that could give us reason to stay in. Even if the trade does work out, optimism bias will try and keep us in even longer than necessary, desperate to grab an extra bit of profit. The problem can strike before we enter, too. A substandard trade setup can look a lot more attractive when optimism bias is hiding the yellow or red flags that should be keeping us out of the market.

Why does the brain do this? Why do we persistently fail to update our beliefs when negative information is available, but apply positive information without difficulty?

Let's take a look at Bob. Bob is an optimist. He has to be. If he was a realist, he would probably be dead already.

Bob is out hunting. It's his main occupation. He has to eat, and he has other mouths to feed back at home in the cave. Today Bob is after a rabbit. He's seen one, and he's been chasing around trying to catch it for the last hour. He's caught rabbits in the past, and knows that they are delicious and that the whole family enjoys Bob's Bunny Bake. But after all his efforts, the rabbit has just disappeared down a hole, well out of reach.

Bob has acquired new information: rabbits can escape. In fact rabbits, being rapid little blighters, probably escape more often than they get caught.

If Bob used this information every time he failed to catch a rabbit, updating his beliefs about his ability to do so, he would soon come to the conclusion that his chances of trapping bunnies are very low indeed. So low, that it would appear futile to even try. Such a belief would lead to a very hungry early human, and weakened from hunger he would be even less successful in his hunting, adding weight to his now overwhelmingly negative outlook on his hunting skills.

You can see where this is going. Evolution has seen to it that no matter how many setbacks Bob encounters in his daily chase, he manages to maintain the belief he will ultimately be successful. And with good reason; even if he only snatches one rabbit in ten, it's probably enough to live on.

Confirmation Bias

Confirmation Bias is the other side of the optimism bias coin. It's another example of selective perception, or the filtering of information. But instead of blocking out data that is detrimental to us, confirmation bias seeks out the positive and boosts it, presenting it to our conscious mind as a front page newsflash with a massive headline. It shouts, *'You were right!'* in no uncertain terms.

Everyone loves to be right, so naturally we take to heart any information that confirms our beliefs, reinforcing them even more. If we are climate change deniers for example, not only does optimism bias filter out all the latest scientific proof of the problem, but its twin sibling confirmation bias will scour the news and pull out anything that supports our view, no matter how tenuous or unsubstantiated the claims.

Here's another example closer to home. We're trying a new trading strategy. We take ten trades. Eight are losers, two are winners. Subconsciously we bury the losers, downplaying their significance. But those two profitable trades we take to heart. We champion them, hold them dear, and use them to boost our belief that the strategy is a keeper, even though the bigger picture says otherwise.

Taken to its logical conclusion, we can end up seeing trades that just aren't there. The merest hint of something that looks like a recent winner has us jumping in with both feet.

The evolutionary reason behind confirmation bias is, of course, the same as that behind optimism bias. Every rabbit that Bob manages to get his hands on enhances his view of his hunting skills, and confirms his belief that bunnies are the perfect lunchtime snack. The two biases work hand in hand to ensure Bob keeps getting out of bed in the morning, and sets off on the daily trek to seek out new warrens. Bob has to believe, for himself, and the future of mankind.

Hack It!

These first two cognitive biases conspire to upset our best efforts when it comes to trading. They hide the truth from us, convincing us that the long trade we just took really is working out, and that the falling price is nothing but a quick retracement. How can we possibly beat something we are inherently blind to?

Actually, it's really simple. The most effective method I have found for seeing what's really on a chart, instead of seeing what I *want* to see, is to turn the chart upside down.

You can do this either physically, or in your head. To start with, I'd recommend physically flipping charts until you get the hang of it, because it stops you cheating yourself.

Turning your charts upside down might sound a little odd, but it's actually incredibly effective because it hijacks our optimism and confirmation biases and uses their power for good.

An example is in order. Let's imagine we see a great setup to go long our preferred stock / future / currency pair / commodity / whatever. We enter our trade, but the price doesn't rise as we expect. According to our strategy as detailed in our trading plan, we should exit now, even if it means taking a loss. We know that losses are part of trading and are to be expected. But optimism bias will work hard to blind us to the signs that the trade is going bad. It will hide the signals that the price is falling.

But if we turn our chart upside down, we can confuse the bias. It knows that we're long, and it will be actively looking for evidence that the price is rising. If it finds it on an upside down chart, it has just been tricked into proving to us that the right way up, the trade must be bad! We have no more excuses for staying in, and can exit quickly with a small loss rather than letting the trade get away from us and turn into a potentially much larger drawdown.

We can use the exact same hack before entering trades, too. It we're studying a chart and are thinking that a long entry looks good, we can try flipping that chart to see if a short trade looks promising. If the upside down chart still looks like a great long, we know our original idea was bad.

Try flipping your charts before every entry. And when in trades, try flipping your charts every so often (how often depends on the timescale you trade) and see if, when upside-down, you're still getting the same signals. If you are, then you know something is wrong.

With practice you can learn to see a chart upside down without physically moving your display. In the meantime, there are a few ways you can rotate the screen, and they depend on the kind of computer you have:

If you have a laptop or tablet computer, the easiest thing is usually just to lift it up and turn it around. You don't need to keep it that way for long, so it's the quickest and simplest method. Tablets like iPads may adjust the image so that it's the right way up again after you rotate the hardware; if that's the case, use your device's rotation lock setting to prevent it happening.

If you have a desktop Windows computer, you probably don't want to be heaving a big monitor upside down. Fortunately most Windows machines can rotate the display with a keyboard shortcut: hold down the Control and Alt keys and press the Up, Down, Left or Right arrow keys to rotate. If that doesn't work, you might need to enable the option in your Display Preferences, which you can find in the Control Panel.

An alternative method for Windows users who can't use the shortcuts, or who don't want to mess about finding the relevant display settings, is to use a software utility instead. Check out this book's *Resources Page* for a link to a free utility.

If you are using a Mac desktop, or don't want to turn your MacBook laptop upside down, you're in luck. OSX has built-in screen rotation, though it's a bit fiddly. Open System Preferences (the gear icon on your dock, or find it by clicking on the Apple symbol in the top left corner). Then hold down the Option and Command keys together and click on Displays. You'll see an option to rotate your display in 90 degree increments; select 180 degrees and then confirm. Note that while the display is flipped the mouse will be upside down too.

Most flavours of Linux are able to rotate the display. The exact method depends on the distribution, and there are too many of those to cover here. If you're a Linux user, your favourite search engine should be able to provide a suitable solution.

If you are trading forex, flipping your charts is really easy; just load up a chart for the opposite currency pair. There's no need to actually turn your computer upside down. For example, if you are looking at a chart of the USD/GBP, you can load up a chart for GBP/USD. You're still looking at the same exchange rate, but upside-down.

Illusory Correlation

What was the weather like the last time you made a really good profitable trade? What, you didn't notice? Quite right too! The weather has as much influence over trading performance as the colour of your eyes. And yet, traders have a tendency to attach mystical powers to all sorts of things when it comes to explaining performance.

It's not just traders, either. In many an interview, former Formula One racing driver David Coulthard has brought up the subject of his lucky underpants. Given to him by his aunt, he won his first few karting races while wearing them. Convinced of their ability to bring good fortune, he continued wearing them for every Formula One race he participated in, until a particularly bad crash rendered them unwearable.

Even after that crash, Coulthard continued to bring his special pants to race meetings, certain that if they were to be left behind he would stand no chance of beating the other drivers to the finish line.

Did these underpants have magical abilities? Of course not. Mr Coulthard was simply a slave to illusory correlation. His subconscious mind made a connection between his aunt's gift and his karting win.

Every subsequent win that occurred while he was wearing the pants only served to reinforce this correlation between underwear and racing performance.

Illusory correlation is particularly toxic because it provides the seeds of poor judgement that are subsequently fed and watered by *optimism* and *confirmation* bias. Coulthard didn't win every race in which he wore his lucky pants, far from it. But every time he *did* win, confirmation bias reinforced the link that illusory correlation first created. And the times he lost, or crashed out? Optimism bias made sure those were quietly forgotten about.

As traders, we're always on the lookout for something that will give us an edge. Sometimes an amazing trade will come along, one that blows all our expectations out of the water. We make an insane — and unexpected — profit, and we're on cloud nine. Once we've calmed down, and perhaps after a few bottles of champagne (if we're one of those types), we go back to the charts and try and figure out what it was that made the trade so special. Was it the time of day? Perhaps the stock, or contract, or currency pair that we traded. We'll focus in on differences, anything that was abnormal about this trade compared to others. Perhaps the position size was bigger or smaller than usual. Maybe, and this is the most dangerous of all, we didn't follow the trading plan to the letter. Or maybe, like Coulthard, we put the success down to our choice of underwear for the day. We'll try and hang our result onto any reason we can find, because that's so much more satisfying than admitting the truth: that sometimes, freak trades just happen.

Attributing success to random events is not dangerous in itself. The real problem comes next time we see a similar set of circumstances. Wearing our lucky pants? Great! Nothing can go wrong. Every trade will be a winner today. We enter with abandon, paying little attention to rhyme or reason.

There's a flip side to illusory correlation, and one that's equally dangerous. It's when we attribute our *failure* to an outside influence. And by outside influence, I mean anything other than us, the trader. We don't like to admit we're wrong, and so we'll try and blame anything except ourselves when a trade doesn't go right. It's so much easier to accept that a trade was a loser because it's raining today, or because the big players were shaking out stops, than because we didn't follow our plan correctly.

It's even more tempting to hang a loss on some arbitrary reasoning when we *did* follow the plan, because that means admitting that sometimes things just don't work out and there's nothing we can do about it. If there's one thing we human beings dislike more than admitting we're wrong, it's admitting that not everything in the world can be explained. It's why there are so many conspiracy theories about everything from the untimely deaths of princesses to government cover-ups about UFOs hiding in military bases.

Illusory correlation is both our enemy and our friend. I dislike the term *frenemy* that gets thrown around by venture capitalist types, but sadly it is pretty accurate when dealing with this particular bias.

We've already seen why illusory correlation can be bad for our wealth, but what possible use can it be?

Well it turns out, correlation is pretty important. Essential, in fact.

Correlation is one of the principle means by which we make new discoveries and acquire new information. I'm not talking about how we learn to read, or do mathematics, or memorise the order of the planets; I'm talking, of course, about how mankind learns anything truly new.

Observe Bob and his extended family for a while, and we can see how they use correlation to discover what is safe to eat, and what isn't. When Aunt Mabel ate those tall red mushrooms from under the bush over there, then keeled over and died an hour later, correlation made sure that the rest of the family stayed well away from the fungi.

When Uncle Horris accidentally knocked over the morning's kill onto the fire, thus discovering the joys of barbecuing, it was correlation that ensured everyone understood why lunch was so tasty that day.

And when sister Sue found that sweeping out the cave was more enjoyable when there was an R in the day? Well that was *illusory* correlation. The spelling of an arbitrary name for a part of the week has no effect on the satisfaction to be gained by performing household chores. But that didn't matter, because it didn't stop the cave from being cleaned regularly.

With massive upside to the development of the species, and relatively little downside, correlation is a big win for evolution.

Hack It!

The solution to this sticky problem can be found in its purpose. Illusory correlation is bad. It can encourage us to make decisions based on arbitrary events or circumstances that have no real influence on the outcome. *Correlation* in and of itself though, is a good thing. It's trying to help us learn, so let's use it to do precisely that.

We need to make correlation work for us. That means dumping the illusions and working with the real reason for our success and failure, which is our ability to execute.

When we exit a trade and make either a profit or loss, our subconscious mind immediately fires up its *correlation engine*. Like a high-powered vacuum cleaner, the engine is going to suck up all available information about the circumstances surrounding the result. And like a vacuum cleaner, it won't be making any judgements about what it should and should not be ingesting. If it happens to notice there's an R in the day, or that it's raining, or that — heaven forbid — we entered the trade two ticks earlier than the trading plan said we should, then all of that information is going to be sucked up and stored away.

What we must do is ensure that we feed our correlation engine with only the information we know to be important. It's not going to filter the good from the bad, so we must.

As traders, we know we can't affect the market, only our ability to execute trades to the best of our ability. So good information would be anything related to our execution. Things like whether we judged the setup correctly, if we entered at the right time, exited according to our own rules, etc.

Noting all of these mentally, in the way we might note that it's a bit chilly for the time of year, isn't enough. We have to force-feed these facts into our subconscious. We must ram them down the throat of the correlation engine, overloading it so that it has no spare capacity to suck up random and irrelevant data.

Fortunately, overloading the engine is pretty easy. We do it by writing down what we want it to learn. Now this is important, and you're going to hate me for this, but I'm going to say it anyway: you have to write this stuff down longhand. No keyboards. A pen and paper. Ideally, in a book.

Forming letters with a pen is a more complex task than hitting a key, so it requires more brain power. It is, cognitively speaking, *more expensive* than typing. The action triggers biological activity within your brain, engaging more neurones than are required to operate a keyboard. When so many neurones are involved in the recording of information longhand, the information is more likely to be stored.

In other words if you write with a pen, you are more likely to remember what it is you wrote.

Not only that, but because your brain is more engaged with the words you are writing, it has less time to spend on unimportant tasks — like vacuuming up irrelevant data that could lead to illusory correlation.

WHAT TO WRITE

I advocate the use of a trading journal. It is essential for hacking illusory correlation, and it can be used to beat other biases too, as we shall see.

The journal should take the form of an exercise book or notebook. You want something where you can write free-form, so diaries aren't usually a good idea as they'll limit the space available for a given day.

Start a new page for each day's trading, noting the date, and anything that might have a material effect on your performance, like ill health or technical problems. *Don't* bother recording the weather, or what you're wearing, or what you had for dinner. If you want to look back fondly on those memories, use a separate journal. This one is all about the trades.

For each trade you enter, I suggest noting the following information at a minimum:

• *What* you are trading. The name of the stock, or future, or currency pair, etc.

• *How* you are trading it. The setup or pattern you are using. If you only trade a single setup then this is redundant, otherwise, come up with a shorthand and standardised way of recording this information. For example, if you trade the strategy from my *How To Day Trade Stocks For Profit* book, you might label your trades as '1234' and 'OR' and 'ERB', etc. It doesn't matter how you do this as long as you stick to your system.

• *Which way* you traded. Long or short.

• *When* you entered.

• *How much* you entered at (price), and any slippage from your target entry price.

• The position *size* you took.

When you exit a trade, you should add the following information:

• The price you exited at.

• The size you exited (if a partial exit).

- *Why* you exited. For example, the stop loss was hit, the target price was hit, or the trade didn't work out.

Trade logging should never become so cumbersome that it takes away from managing your positions, but the above information shouldn't take more than 30 seconds to write down longhand. It doesn't need to be recorded the instant you are in the trade, managing the position is always more important.

Here's an example of how I would log one of my stock day trades:

```
OR, L, QCOM
IN 09:45 1000 @ 64.47 (1)
OUT 10:10 1000 @ 64.94, Target
4/5 (exited too late)
```

This is telling me that I traded an OR pattern (one of my regulars), I went long (L), and the stock I was trading was QCOM. These three pieces of information can be written down before even entering the trade, while I watch the chart set up. If the pattern doesn't confirm and I choose not to enter, that's valuable information and I could write down why I decided to let the trade pass.

In this case though, I did enter. The time, price, and size are noted, as is the 1 cent slippage I got on my entry (1).

The exit time, price, and size are recorded, along with the reason for getting out, which in this case was because the price had reached the target the setup anticipated.

There's something after that too, and it's a really important bit of information:

```
4/5 (exited too late)
```

This is my *execution score*. It's a score I award myself for how well I think I followed my trading plan. A five out of five would mean I did everything exactly right. In this example, I knocked off a point because I was a bit slow on the exit, which resulted in losing a few cents on the trade as the price retraced.

Scoring yourself in this way forces you to think about what really matters — the execution — rather than what doesn't. You'll see I haven't noted whether the trade was profitable or a loss. It's easy enough to work out from the entry and exit price, but it's not important information at the time of logging. All I want to know, and all I want my correlation engine to take notice of, is how well I followed my trading plan.

There's More to Logging

Even if you never look at your trade log again, it will be beneficial to you. Remember, the physical act of writing the notes on the paper will cause biological activity in your brain that directs your correlation engine to take notice of what matters, leaving it no time to create any illusory correlation.

In fact, there's more we can do with a trading log, and we'll see how as we investigate other ways in which your brain is trying to hijack your trading.

Apophenia

As I write this chapter, it's getting on for the end of August. Everyone is on holiday (except me!). Government is running on tick over, the television is showing endless repeats, and I've more chance of visiting Mars than I have of getting a plumber to come out and fix a leaky pipe. It's the summer doldrums, and nowhere is that more evident than in the newspapers. It's at this time of year that I can almost guarantee I will see a headline like this:

Second coming of Christ:

Slice of toast bears face of Jesus himself.

Yes, that's an actual headline from a real newspaper. It's the kind of cranky story the papers like to run when there's no actual news happening anywhere.

This particular article goes on to explain how a 24-year-old man from Manchester, England, was baffled when his slice of bread popped out of his toaster bearing the likeness of Jesus burnt into its side. His friend wasn't so convinced. Apparently he thought it looked more like Ozzy Osborne — a convenient twist to a familiar tale, rendering it fit for publication despite countless versions of the same basic report being run year in year out.

So what's going on? Have these men, and hundreds or thousands of other people before them, received divine messages on the side of their preferred breakfast snack? The accompanying picture in the paper certainly looks like a face on the side of a piece of cooked bread. But of course it's not a face, it's a random pattern of scorch marks that just happens to resemble one. The fact that both men believe it is a face is down to a bias called *apophenia*. They're seeing patterns which aren't really there.

When the patterns in question are found in visual or audible stimuli, such as the image on the side of the toast, scientists call this specific form of apophenia *pareidolia*. If you've ever thought you could see a face in a cloud, or that a rock formation looked suspiciously like a squirrel, then you've experienced pareidolia. But apophenia goes much further than seeing a man in the moon, or a deity on toast. In fact, it's something we experience almost every day.

Ever had a morning like this? You wake up two minutes before the alarm clock goes off. You bounce out of bed feeling refreshed and full of energy. The coffee machine seems to get your brew out quicker than normal. Your journey to work goes as smoothly as possible; you don't encounter a single red light on your way to the station, your train is on time, you get a great seat, and there are no delays. You get off the train, someone hands you a free scratch-card, and when you remove the foil you discover you've won a weekend away. You stroll into your office, the boss smiles and offers to buy you breakfast. You think to yourself, *'I'm having a lucky day today, he probably wants to give me a raise.'*

Now imagine if the opposite happens. You sleep through your alarm, the coffee machine breaks down, and every traffic light is against you, meaning you miss your train. Instead you get one that's packed, runs slow due to engineering works, and the air conditioning is broken. You run the last stretch of your commute from the station to your place of work, making up your delay. As you sprint across a road your phone falls out of your pocket and is run over by a truck. You finally get to your desk only just on time, out of breath, hot, sweaty, and fed up.

When your boss smiles and invites you out for breakfast, do you think about a raise? Or might you more likely think, *'I'm having a terrible day, he's probably going to tell me I'm fired!'*

In either case, any attribution of *luck* to your morning would obviously be erroneous; there's no such thing. Equally, to try and predict the reason for your boss's breakfast invitation based on the way your day has gone so far, though tempting, would be quite ridiculous. The boss has no knowledge of your troublesome commute. Yet we all do this sort of thing, because we're all human and we're all programmed to look for patterns, even where none can possibly exist.

In fact, the human brain is a pattern recognition super-computer, and it has good reason to be. *Correlation* helps us discover new information, but pattern recognition takes that ability and turbo-charges it, allowing us to make new discoveries based on only partial information, and even to make predictions about the world.

For example, when Aunt Mabel popped her clogs after munching the tall red mushrooms, correlation meant everyone in Bob's family stayed well away from them. But now her sister, Aunt Dorris, has found some other red mushrooms. These are flat and round, a completely different shape from those that did for Mabel. She sautés them and enjoys them for lunch. Sadly, it is her last meal. Now Bob has two pieces of information, and if he's smart, he might notice that although they look different, both types of mushroom were red. He doesn't need to experience the death of another family member to know that it's best to steer well clear of all shapes of red mushroom that he might discover when out foraging.

Pattern recognition then, is a vital skill, and one that has kept us alive long enough for us to be discussing it here.

Most of the time, it's better for us to see patterns that aren't really there than it is to miss patterns that are. Most of the time, apophenia is just mildly amusing, a good source of stories for slow news days, or funny pictures to post on Twitter. It is, however, problematic for traders, because we're actively looking for patterns.

A large part of our skill as traders lies in our ability to spot predictable behaviour, be it technical shapes or formations on price charts, or fundamental shifts in data about a company or market or currency. Patterns are our business. Anything that interferes with our capacity to determine real ones from false is going to be detrimental to our performance.

Forcing ourselves to see chart patterns that aren't really there, or aren't properly or fully formed, is an obvious and common example. I call this *squinting*, and it's particularly prevalent among novice traders. Our desire to find good trade setups revs up our pattern recognition system and sends it into overdrive. Suddenly everything looks like a great potential trade — *if* you half close your eyes and look at it just so.

Apophenia brings other problems for traders though, regardless of whether they use technicals, fundamentals, or both. We've all experienced bad runs, taking loss after loss, even when we stick rigidly to our plan. When that happens, it's very easy to start coming up with reasons why. We tell ourselves that the market makers are trying to take out stops. We start to wonder if our broker is deliberately messing with our orders to try and wheedle more commissions. We even go as far as to convince ourselves that we're having a run of bad luck.

All these negative — and flawed — ideas are dangerous. I call them the *monsters*, because like mythical beasts, they can terrify us, even though they don't really exist.

There's no such thing as luck. It would be professional suicide for our broker to fiddle with our orders. Market makers don't go hunting for stops, or engineering fakeouts, or doing any of the other underhand shenanigans that new traders think go on. Sometimes, trades just don't work out. And as with any random distribution of data, sometimes a few losses will happen in close proximity. If we assign meaning to them, we are in danger of withdrawing from the market. If we believe the broker is out to screw us, it makes sense to walk away. Yet in almost every case that would be completely the wrong thing to do, because it means we won't be there to profit from the trade that does go right. And as long as we're executing correctly, and trading a solid strategy with positive expectancy, then that trade will happen. We have to be there to profit from it.

Before we move on, a quick word on the subject of luck. I don't believe in it, and if you want to succeed as a trader, neither should you. My dictionary defines the word as meaning *success or failure apparently brought by chance rather than through one's own actions*. It goes on to define *chance* as meaning *the occurrence of events in the absence of any obvious intention or cause*.

To suggest that luck plays a part in success or failure would imply that our own intentions and actions have no effect on our results, which is obviously ridiculous. Certainly we cannot control everything when we trade, and there is no doubt that we can execute perfectly and still make losing trades. Does this mean we are experiencing bad luck? No, it just means that markets are unpredictable.

There is an uncontrollable element in every trade (i.e. other market participants), and that introduces an aspect of randomness. Sometimes that randomness brings a string of losses when we might not expect them to occur, and we are tempted to call this *bad luck*. A better definition might be an unfortunate confluence of negative random effects! Similarly, we can execute poorly, but find favourable outcomes brought on by the random element. But to call this unmerited success *lucky* would be dangerous. It would imply that an external force is influencing the outcome of our efforts in a positive manner. Such thinking (a perfect example of apophenia) is what makes traders take unnecessary risks. If you ever find yourself thinking '*I feel lucky,*' step away from the keyboard and think carefully about what that idea really implies.

Hack It!

Let's deal with squinting first. There's a very easy way to avoid this problem, and it's done by subverting another cognitive bias — *contrast bias*. Because we haven't covered that yet, I'm going to leave explaining the hack until later. Trust me, it's worth the wait.

This leaves us with the monsters — the unseen evils that lurk behind the computer, interfering with our orders. Those pesky stop-hunting market makers, those commission-stealing brokers, those— *"But monsters don't exist, Harvey!"* I hear you cry.

Correct! Congratulations, you've just defeated apophenia.

For today.

Next time you have a bad run though, next time a brilliant trade that should have made your fortune appears to shake you out, only to go on and do great things without you, apophenia is going to creep up and bite you again. Which is why you need to be ready for it. You must protect yourself so that when the attack happens, you can hold it off.

There is an almost impenetrable shield that I use against the monsters. That shield is education.

It's pretty obvious when you think about it. The way to put a child's mind at rest about the monster under the bed is to show them there's nothing under the bed. You can defeat the trading monsters in the same way. Peer behind the screen. See for yourself that there's nothing to be afraid of. Educate yourself about the mechanics of the market.

If you possibly can, try and visit a brokerage firm, ideally the one you trade with. Talk to the brokers, meet the market makers. Discover first hand how their jobs work, and why it is absolutely not in their interests (and indeed is nigh-on impossible) to shake out your trades or engineer prices to hit your stops. Prove to yourself beyond all reasonable doubt that the playing field is level. This alone will keep the monsters at bay 90% of the time.

Only 90%? Yes, because your shield will fade over time. It might take days, it might take weeks or months, but eventually the memory of what you have learnt will pale. When that happens, doubts will creep in, creating fissures in your shield. As every child knows, the monsters can find a way through the smallest crack in your armour! That is why education must be backed up with revision.

Before you run away screaming, with memories of revising for high-school exams haunting you, let me just say that revision in this instance is easy. Really easy. In fact, it shouldn't take you more than sixty seconds per day, or even per week, if like me you're really lazy.

My revision works like this. As part of my trading plan I have a pre-market routine. Most of that is stuff like checking where the indices are, looking at market sentiment, reading the news, all that sort of thing. There's another item on my checklist though, and it's to read off a few affirmations. Just a couple of one-liners that I say out loud, to remind myself of the things I know to be true.

For example, before I open up my charts I might say aloud: "The market has no memory. There is no such thing as luck. I am an insignificant player. Nobody is out to get me; nobody else even knows what I'm doing." You get the gist… The actual wording changes from time to time, to take account of where the cracks in my shield are appearing. The text is written into my plan, and I actively check off having read it aloud as a precursor to the trading day.

These affirmations serve a dual purpose. Firstly, they remind me of the things I know to be true. They are shield maintenance. They reinforce the knowledge I have about the mechanics of the market, and in doing so they close up any fissures and prevent the monsters from finding a way in.

Secondly, they program my brain to actively filter out apophenia. They are a form of neural linguistic programming (NLP), a powerful tool that can change the way we think just by what we say. The funny thing about NLP is you don't even have to believe what you are saying for it to have an effect, if you say it often enough. Which means if you don't want to take the time to educate yourself (though I strongly recommend you do), just using positive affirmations like this will, over time, provide you with a shield against the monsters of apophenia.

Feel free to use the above affirmations, or better still, come up with your own. In your trading log, at the end of each day, make a note of any doubts, fears, or worries that occurred to you as you were working. Re-read these notes from time to time. If necessary, educate yourself to dispel anything you can disprove. Then write new affirmations that you can use to defeat your own personal monsters.

NLP is a pretty vast topic, and these sorts of affirmations are the tip of a powerful iceberg. If you're interested in taking brain hacking beyond just improving your trading performance, NLP is a great way to go.

Outcome Bias

I'll mention this one for completeness, but there's no need to go into detail, because outcome bias is such a close relation of optimism and confirmation bias and illusory correlation. It is, essentially, the combined effect of all three.

Outcome bias is our tendency to judge our decisions based on their outcome, rather than the quality of the decisions themselves.

We've all entered trades that we know are substandard. Occasionally, through a confluence of random effects, some of those trades turn out to be profitable. Because of the aforementioned biases, we are prone to modify our view of the entry we took, rating it as good instead of poor. We congratulate ourselves for the good trade instead of reprimanding ourselves for our poor judgement in having entered at all.

The danger is that next time such a substandard setup comes along, we will be much more inclined to take it, even though in reality nothing has changed. There is no greater chance of the trade being profitable than there was before. A substandard setup is still substandard.

Hacking the other three biases will stop outcome bias in its tracks.

Hyberbolic Discounting

Pop quiz: You and I meet up in a pub. After a few drinks I delve into my pocket and pull out a bunch of crisp banknotes. I count out two hundred dollars (or the equivalent in your local currency) and lay the cash out on the table. "This money is for you. I want you to have it," I say.

Naturally you are sceptical, but this being a fictional example, you don't ask too many questions. You reach out to take the money, but before your fingers touch the green, I snatch it away again. "You can have this now," I say, waving the bunch of notes under your nose, "or you can leave now without the cash, we can meet up here again one year from now, and I will give you five hundred dollars instead."

Which option do you choose?

If you choose to take the money and run, you are probably employing hyperbolic discounting.

If we used our vortex manipulators to go forwards rather than backwards, say, twelve months from now, we could observe the future you. That you might well be thinking with regret about the extra money you would have had if you had waited it out. This is what hyperbolic discounting boils down to: making a decision now about the value of something that the future you might regret later.

The words hyperbola and hyperbole both come from the Greek word for *excessive*. In the case of hyperbolic discounting, the excess in question is the value placed on immediate gain in relation to long-term gain. We have a tendency to over-value what's on offer now compared to what's available later.

In the above example, if you waited twelve months you could more than double the money I'm offering you. All things being equal, logically you're better off waiting the year. But the desire for instant gratification, the thought of having the readies in your hands *right now*, outweighs the advantages of having more later.

Mortgage companies like to use this trick, selling loans loaded with up-front discounts or low fixed-interest rates for the first few years. These promotions are almost always offset with a slightly higher rate for the rest of the term, and if you calculate the total payments for the life of the mortgage, the difference can be stunning compared to a regular deal. Yet when we're faced with a choice of extra money in our pocket now — especially when buying a home, which is always an expensive time — versus a saving ten, fifteen or twenty years down the road, most people will choose the discount.

Interestingly, the effect diminishes with time. Imagine that after plonking my banknotes down on the table, our pub conversation went like this: "I'm not offering you any money today, but if you come back here in eleven months' time, I'll give you this two hundred dollars. You don't even have to buy a round, the cash will be yours. But if you come back in twelve months' time, I'll give you five hundred." The chances are you would opt to wait the extra month. One month longer to more than double the money is a no-brainer, right? Yet waiting a year to gain five hundred dollars is exactly what was most likely rejected in the first scenario!

The effect of hyperbolic discounting on our trading should be obvious. When we're sitting watching the screen and our trade is showing a good paper profit, we have an overwhelming urge to exit and take that profit now, rather than wait until our strategy says we *should* exit, which could result in a much larger gain later on. The desire for a quick profit outweighs the better result we could have if we could be a bit more patient. Not only that, but we don't want to risk losing what we've made so far (*loss aversion*), so we're even more willing to sacrifice the potentially greater profit available if we were to stay in.

The longer we think we need to stay in the trade, the less value we place on the potential future profit. For example, if we made $100 in the first ten minutes of a trade, and our strategy suggested that an extra hour staying in could add another $100 to the pot, the additional time doesn't seem worth the effort and the risk. We'd rather take the money we've already made and start looking for the next quick win elsewhere. It's the exact opposite of what we need to do in order to succeed long term as traders. We know we must run winning trades as long as possible to extract the maximum profit. It's logical, and our brain is perfectly okay with that fact as we sit here and think about it happening some arbitrary time in the future. But once we're actually in a winning trade, we're much higher up the hyperbolic curve. We've got profit right now, and the potential extra cash seems a long way off. Subconsciously we discount its value massively. It just doesn't seem worth the risk.

As with all cognitive biases, the reason we desire instant gratification comes down to being hard wired to meet our physiological needs before all else.

Back in 50,000 BC, Bob is out hunting with his buddies again. He and his team know that there's a herd of deer that come by the local watering hole every evening, just before dusk. Early in the morning they set up camp behind some bushes (they want to get the best spot before other tribes turn up). To their immense surprise, shortly before lunchtime, and with their bellies rumbling, they see a lone deer drinking from the watering hole. They could let it pass, wait hours longer until the whole herd comes along, and then try and catch five or six deer. On the other hand, they could just jump this single defenceless creature right now, get the barbecue going, and have a lazy afternoon. After all, there's no guarantee that the herd will turn up later. And if it does, they could be competing with six other tribes to catch a few deer. They'll also be weaker by the evening, because they won't have eaten anything.

Of course they're going after the ready-meal that's just walked out in front of them. Instant gratification means they're sure to live to see another day.

Hack It!

Hyperbolic discounting is a flawed ability to judge *value* over *time.* There's not much we can do about the time part — unfortunately my vortex manipulator is purely fictional. We can hack our value system though. If we can remove the concept of profit from the trade, we won't have a problem evaluating it.

In fact, doing away with the idea of profit avoids a whole heap of problems, not just hyperbolic discounting. It's a big topic, too big to discuss here, so I'm going to show you exactly how to do it later, in the section on *Hacking The Reward System.* Feel free to skip ahead if you're impatient. Unlike exiting a trade early, leaving this chapter before its conclusion won't preclude you from jumping back and catching up on what you missed.

Irrational Escalation

My mother-in-law recently discovered eBay. She loves it. She finds all sorts of stuff she never knew she needed, but because the bidding starts at next to nothing, she convinces herself she has to have it.

Inevitably, as the auction draws to a close she finds herself competing with one or two other bidders, driving up the price of her useless article until the clock ticks over, bidding closes, and someone walks away (usually her, it has to be said), having paid more than the article would have cost brand new from a local store.

What's this got to do with trading? Quite a lot, as it turns out. Because the same instinct that causes people to overpay in an auction also drives traders to chase after profits from a losing trade.

I was as guilty of this as anyone in my early days in the markets. I would find a great setup that perfectly matched the criteria in my trading plan. I would enter perfectly with great timing, and get a nice fill with no slippage. Things might start out well, but then the price would turn around and go against me.

Rather than accept that the trade wasn't working out and exit with a small loss, my *optimism bias* would convince me that because the setup was good, the trade had to work out in the end. I told myself that it would come right. And so I would *buy more*, doubling down on my position in order to cover my losses and still make a profit when the price, surely, turned around. But the price almost never turned around, and my *irrational escalation* of my position size meant I lost even more than I would have done had I just stuck to the plan.

To make matters worse, on the very rare occasion the price did turn back, *confirmation bias* would reinforce the idea that the escalation of my position size had been the right thing to do, thus ensuring I continued with this spiral of loss.

Why do we do this? As usual, Bob shows us the answer. He's after another bunny. The poor lad hasn't eaten for a couple of days. Never mind the upper levels of Maslow's hierarchy, Bob needs protein and if he doesn't get some soon, esteem and self-actualisation will be the least of his worries.

He's got one in his sights, but the little blighter's been eating too many vitamin-rich carrots and is faster than any other rabbit in town. Every time Bob makes his move, the bunny outruns him.

The smart idea would probably be to leave this racy rabbit to its own devices and go in search of slower-moving prey. The risk is that all the more lethargic *leporidae* are off sleeping in a burrow, and won't be found before Bob expires of exhaustion. He *has* to chase the one he can see, to the exclusion of all else. It's his best chance.

Hack It!

We are not Bob. We are not dependent on a single kill in order to survive. No trade is worth losing our stake for. Indeed, we know we must keep our losses to a minimum.

Like hyperbolic discounting, irrational escalation is a weakness in our ability to evaluate worth. We lose sight of what's important (the execution of our trading strategy) and chase after what's not (a profit from the trade we are in). So like hyperbolic discounting, the way to hack this bias is to remove the valuation element altogether. Make our job about execution, and let the profits take care of themselves. At the risk of repeating myself, we'll examine a great way to do that later in *Hacking The Reward System*.

Heuristics

In this section we're going to look at a subset of cognitive biases called *psychological heuristics*. A quick definition is in order:

Simple, efficient rules which people often use to form judgments and make decisions.

That's heuristics in a nutshell; rules for helping us make decisions. Mental shortcuts, if you like.

We may not realise it but we use psychological heuristics all the time, including when we trade. Our brains, ever eager to conserve energy, are always on the lookout for ways to avoid work. Making choices requires a lot of effort, so anything that can bypass that effort is welcome.

Unfortunately the shortcuts come with some drawbacks. Whilst most of the time they can and will lead us to a satisfactory decision, when it comes to some activities — trading among them — *satisfactory* isn't good enough. Worse, sometimes these mental shortcuts lead us to decisions that are just plain wrong. However, the fact that they are right more often than they are wrong means that they have stuck around. They've become part of the furniture of the subconscious; we don't notice they're there.

That doesn't mean they can't be beaten though.

Let's dive in and take a look at these heuristics, see how they undermine our best efforts to make good trading decisions, and how we can hack them.

Contrast Bias

A real estate agent was showing me a series of houses one day. We'd got four viewings booked, two in the morning, two after lunch. By the time we sat down to eat at midday, I was feeling rather deflated. My hopes of finding the kind of property I was after were drastically reduced, having visited two dreadful doer-uppers. As I munched on my main course, I was already re-evaluating the merit of my initial brief to the agent, which had included something along the lines of: "I don't mind if the place needs a bit of work doing." It appeared that we did not share the same definition of the word *bit*. The houses we had seen could best be described as ruins. It was more a case of rebuilding than retouching.

Things didn't improve much with the third viewing, a crumbling wreck of a property located right next to a busy road, something I had specifically said was a no-no.

"Don't worry, Mr Walsh," the agent said to me as we climbed back in the car after I had given the place the most honest evaluation that I could politely get away with. He smiled at me. "I know you're going to just love the next one."

I wasn't convinced, but the day was drawing to a close and the last viewing wasn't far away. Perhaps my optimism bias kept me hanging in there.

We drove a short distance, and pulled up in front of what, at the time, looked like a mansion fit for minor royalty.

Thinking the house we had come to see must be hidden around the corner, I got out of the car and started walking further up the road. The agent, amused, called after me. He waved the keys and pointed to the door of the palatial property. Before we even got inside, I was sold.

In hindsight, the house was not what I was looking for. It was still too close to the road. It needed much more work than I was willing to take on. And the garden was too small.

Had we visited this house before all the others, I would have dismissed it out of hand.

But the agent was smart. He knew all about *contrast bias*. He was well aware that by showing this relatively acceptable property after a string of derelict dumps, it would seem much nicer than it really was.

Had he lumped the final house in with some other similarly average dwellings, my day would have ended with me getting back onto the internet to start my search over again. Yet because the agent was clever enough to lower my expectations with substandard properties first, he led me down his carefully prepared path to the house that he wanted to sell me all along. My contrast bias took one look at the place, compared it to the most recently available data about what else was on the market — i.e. the ruins we had spent the rest of the day looking at — and hey presto, I was ready to sign on the dotted line almost before stepping inside. He made the decision so easy that there wasn't really a decision at all.

It's not just real estate agents who know all about contrast bias. High school girls have also been known to employ its power. A staple of teen angst movies, the horrific 'ugly friend syndrome' is, sadly, a reality. An average-looking girl chooses to hang out with a friend who is somewhat chubbier or less classically 'attractive' than herself, knowing that when seen together, she will appear more desirable. It's all subjective of course, but there's no doubt that it happens.

Traders are not immune to contrast bias. Far from it. We can sit in front of a monitor and watch choppy charts move sideways all day long, waiting patiently for a decent setup to come along. And when a *half*-decent setup comes along, one that, had it occurred first thing in the morning we would have let pass because it wasn't up to our high standards, we jump on it with glee. Compared to the dross that we've been watching for hours, the substandard potential trade seduces us with its limited appeal. Only later, when we're reviewing what went wrong, will we see it for the fixer-upper it really was.

Contrast bias is one of our most commonly employed heuristics. We use it all the time because it's cognitively very cheap, and it has a high degree of success. Its very effectiveness is what makes it so pervasive, and so dangerous to traders. So where did this shortcut for decision making come from? Why is it we are so keen to compare and contrast what is in front of us to the exclusion of other data? Let's pop back to the Middle Paleolithic period for a moment.

Bob is a busy man. There are only so many hours of daylight in which to get his chores done. He has to get his family up and ready for school, he has to go and catch some rabbits for lunch, before then doing the washing up, helping Mrs Bob clean the cave, and getting a fire lit before it gets dark. With a bit of luck, he'll just have time for a glass of home-brewed beer on the veranda with his mates (pubs haven't been invented yet) before it's too dangerous to be outside.

All of this means that when Bob is out hunting, he can't waste too much time deciding what he's going to try and catch.

Bob's in his favourite rabbit-catching patch, and it looks like he's in luck. There's a nice fat juicy rabbit sitting to his left, and a slightly skinnier specimen on his right. He needs to choose which way he's going fast, before the bunnies both bounce off. He's not going to waste time and mental energy trying to work out whether the fat rabbit really is the best he can hope for today. Thinking is expensive, it burns precious calories. The kids will be home for lunch soon, and he really does fancy that beer tonight. Bob's choice is an easy one to make. He turns left, and raises his spear.

Contrast bias gave Bob a way to reach rapid decisions without expending valuable time or effort. With the limited data of what was available at any given moment, he could make snap choices. They might not have been the best possible choices — there could be a better bunny just around the corner — but they were usually good enough to keep him fed and safe.

Most of the time contrast bias gets it right. Bob catches the bigger rabbit, so he and his kids don't go hungry. The problems arise if he gets lazy and relies too much on its charms. What if Bob always chooses the bigger of the first two rabbits he sees, but all of those rabbits are getting smaller over time? Eventually he will be hunting tiny creatures that don't have enough meat on them to feed even his youngest child. If he never stops to think that there might be a more substantial meal behind the next bush, his family will become malnourished and weak.

It's worth noting that we make contrast bias comparisons both spatially and temporally. Bob was contrasting two rabbits that were within his field of vision (a spatial comparison), but it could equally be that he has seen a couple of scrawny subjects pass him by earlier, and now there's a single more robust specimen on offer. The contrast is made against those most recently seen rabbits (a temporal comparison). Delving any further back in his memory — to consider yesterday's much better meal for example — would be time consuming and energy intensive.

As traders, it's this temporal contrast bias that is so often our downfall. On a slow day, it's too easy to fall into the trap of thinking that a badly formed setup or a suboptimal stock is the perfect trading opportunity when all we've seen all day is choppy charts and low volume.

Hack It!

Contrast bias is a sneaky customer. It creeps up on us over time, wheedling its way into our decisions little by little. At the end of a long day, particularly one without much action, we are weakened against its charms.

Happily for us though, it's a very easy bias to subvert. We can flip contrast bias a full one hundred and eighty degrees and have it improve every trading decision we make. And as a bonus, when we hack contrast bias, we'll also be overcoming a large part of the *apophenia* problem, too.

The way we do so is by building a library of model trades. With a set of perfect text-book examples for each setup we ever plan to trade, we can compare every chart we see against the best of the best.

At the end of a long day with only choppy sideways charts, the first hint of a setup that comes along will be very appealing, because we're comparing it to the junk that came before. But if we hold up a model of what a perfect setup should look like, now our contrast bias is obliged to make the comparison with that instead. If the trade looks good against the model, then we're on. But if it shows it up for the ugly friend it really is, then we've just saved ourselves from a costly loss.

Keep your model trade library right next to your main trading screen. When you see a potential trade setting up, find the model for that pattern and physically hold it up against the screen so you can compare side by side. If you trade based on fundamentals rather than technicals, you can adapt your trade library accordingly.

Care must be taken not to go to extremes with this hack. When you compare every trade to perfection, your potential trades can all end up looking substandard. If you find your model trade library is preventing you from entering anything at all, then consider dumbing it down. Back off and replace perfection with *good enough* trade examples. Instead of contrasting your setup with the best of the best, compare with the minimum acceptable standard. Anything which comes along that's better than your model will be a no-brainer — take it. Tweaking your model library like this is a fine line to walk, but the rewards are well worth the effort.

To start your library, look back through your trading records, call up historical charts, and pick the best. It doesn't matter if they're not A1 model trades, you can add to and improve it over time, switching out better chart examples as you encounter them.

Social Proof

Imagine you're driving down the highway, it's gone midday, and you've been on the road for hours. You're tired, thirsty, hungry, and in need of a comfort break too. It's time to stop, stretch your legs, and have some lunch. So you begin looking for a diner.

Fortunately you don't have to wait too long, and after about ten minutes of empty road you find two diners right opposite each other, one either side of the road. At first glance the diners look much the same. They're both a similar size, they're built in the same style, they're both clean and tidy, and they're both open for business. In fact, there's only one obvious difference between them. The diner on the right has about twenty cars in the car park. The diner on the left has a single vehicle stopped outside.

You're slowing down, and there's a queue of traffic behind you, already honking their horns impatiently, waiting for you to get out of the way. Which way are you going to turn? Which diner do you choose?

Most people, given a choice like this, will turn right. Some of those people will be able to tell you why, some won't. For those who can explain their decision, it will usually be something like: "The right-hand diner must be better, because it's busy." Or, "Nobody is eating in the left-hand diner, so there must be something wrong with it."

Makes sense, doesn't it? All those people eating in the busy diner must know something we don't, otherwise they wouldn't be there.

Basing decisions on the actions of other people in this way is called *social proof*, sometimes also called the *bandwagon effect*. We see something happening and we jump on the bandwagon, without really thinking about our decision. The social proof heuristic says to us, *'If it's good enough for all those people, it must be good enough for me.'* Our brain, having made a nice easy choice, can go back to sleep.

But was it really the right choice? Do all those people parked up outside the busy diner really know something we don't? What if, just an hour ago, there was only one car outside each of the two diners. Perhaps the next customer who drove down the road chose to stop at the right-hand diner on a whim. That diner now had two cars outside.

The next car along after that also slowed down, making a choice about where to eat. Perhaps he, like us, thought that the diner with two cars was a better prospect. Twice as many customers as the left-hand diner; perhaps it was more sought after and had a better reputation. Now that diner had three cars in the car park. When the fourth traveller rolled up, it was looking even more popular.

Before we know it, the right-hand diner had filled up with people who have *never eaten there before*, but who believed that it must be a good place to stop because so many others were already there. Apart from the first one or two customers, who chose mostly by chance, all the subsequent customers could have made their decision based purely on social proof.

It's entirely possible that the left-hand diner offers far better food at much more reasonable prices, but it doesn't matter because everyone was making decisions on auto-pilot. The next day, it could be the left-hand diner that will get lucky and attract those first few customers, thus ensuring it becomes the number one spot for lunch.

When you know about social proof, you start to see it everywhere. Go to any market and you'll see some stalls that are really busy, attracting a large crowd. And you'll see some that are completely empty. People will walk right past those empty stalls without so much as a glance, but they'll push and shove to see what's being sold at the popular ones. We hate to miss out. If you want to try a fun experiment, grab a couple of friends and go and stand at an empty market stall and coo over whatever it is they're selling. See how long it takes you to attract a crowd. I guarantee, it won't be long.

It's easy to see where social proof came from and how it's helped us as a species. When Bob went out looking for rabbits, he probably had a few favourite places where he hung out, knowing that he had a reasonable chance of getting lucky. He would pick one of those spots, then sit around and wait for a bunny to pop up out of a hole. But if Bob happened to see a whole load of his cave-buddies crowding around one particular warren, there would be a good chance they knew something he didn't. So rather than wasting time hanging around in random spots, Bob could join his friends. Energy saved, Bob's survival more or less assured.

The interesting thing about social proof as it applies to trading is that this particular cognitive bias is so pervasive and so powerful, it can move markets. It's part of what actually makes prices move.

We know that — giant auto-trading computers aside — markets are made of people like us taking positions based on our opinion of future price movements. When enough people take similar positions, the price moves. And when the price moves, more traders jump on the *bandwagon*. When patterns start to form, things really kick up a gear. We see a perfect triangle pattern appear, or a support line break, and we're all in there like a shot. The pattern is basically social proof, charted.

So in some respects social proof is our friend. It's a big part of what lets us do our job. But like all the biases, it has a dark side. In fact, it has two.

The first works a bit like this. You're watching a price chart, patiently waiting for your favourite trading pattern to come along. The price is rising nicely, and there's a pretty strong uptrend playing out. The market sentiment is upbeat, the mood upbeat. Maybe the futures are rising, as are all the sector indices. You get that distinct feeling that prices are headed north for the foreseeable future. And then the price on your chart really takes off. Volume goes through the roof, and the ticker explodes in a frenzy of action. You have no idea why this is happening, but you feel an intense urge to be part of it. Money is being made hand over first by your (probably unseen) peers, and you want some of it. Your trading plan goes out of the window, and you jump in with both feet, following the crowd for no other reason than because they are a crowd.

Perhaps, if you're lucky, you make some money. Good for the account balance, bad for your head. *Confirmation bias* will ram home the idea that you were right to take the off-plan trade. But we've all been here, and we all know that most of the time, volatile moves that we don't understand rarely end well. When the crowd, who may or may not know why they are getting into this trade, decide it's time to exit, you don't want to be the last trader standing. If you don't know why you're getting in, better just not to get in.

There's another dark side to social proof in trading, and it can happen even when you're not actually trading. It can creep up on you and upset your entire trading plan, and you don't see it happening because when it does, you convince yourself that you are improving your trading education.

I'm talking about chatrooms and forums.

Don't get me wrong, forums in all their guises (and I include Twitter and Facebook groups and all the other fancy social media platforms) are an amazing resource. I suspect a great many people reading this book would never had got into trading in the first place if it hadn't been for trading forums. Never in the history of mankind has it been easier to think of a subject and start learning about it within minutes.

The problems with these resources aren't about the learning process per se (although there are some of those too), but more about their utility when you have got the basics down and have a good solid trading plan to work from. The forums can hijack your efforts in two ways.

Outside of trading hours, they tempt you with fancy new setups or trading ideas. We've probably all been through what I call the *grail hunt* period of our trading careers. It's the part where we convince ourselves that there must be a magical Holy Grail trading strategy that always wins, or that loses so infrequently that it hardly notices. We persuade ourselves that the reason we're not profitable yet is because we haven't found that system, or that at the very least, our system isn't good enough. All those other super-profitable traders in the forums must know at least one secret we have yet to discover. So we keep mining the old threads looking for it.

Eventually we get past the grail hunt stage when we realise that there is no perfect system. The only 'secret' the profitable traders on the forums know is that you need a few reliable, positive expectancy setups and excellent discipline to trade them, and the money follows.

But we still get tempted. It's so easy to pop in to a group of traders online or see a mega-thread on a bulletin board where everyone is discussing an incredible new indicator or an amazing new pattern. Our social proof heuristic kicks in; they must know something we don't, and we don't want to miss out. So we join the group, have a peek at what they're all taking about, and then have a go ourselves. Sometimes it's good, and it works out. More often than not though, we just end up derailing our own plan. I've lost count of the number of student traders I've seen try out new setups, only to dump them at the end of the week then look back at their week's trading log and see how much profit they missed out on by not sticking to their own proven formula.

Inside of trading hours, the social platforms conspire to take your focus away from your plan too, but in real time. The chatrooms and Twitter are the absolute worst for this. If you allow yourself to watch them, it's almost impossible not to get drawn in to following other people's trades. When your chatroom or timeline bursts into life with everyone jumping into the same stock or currency pair or whatever, can you ignore the pull? Can you sit on the sidelines, watching them have all the fun? Some people can, but they are in the minority.

Following other traders can be a valuable learning tool, but in the right time and place. Otherwise it's just a distraction, and one we quickly come to regret.

Hack It!

Let's deal with the chatrooms and forums first. These are easy to handle — in theory. You simply stay away from them during trading hours. If you're reliant on a trading room to make your decisions for you, then you're not a real trader anyway, you're just a clone. You might as well close your trading account and put your funds into a managed investment account. It's the same principle and you don't need to do the work of placing the trades. Real traders don't need to be watching any kind of social media (unless, I suppose, you have figured out a trading strategy that makes decisions based on the activity of a large group of people, which isn't the same thing as following individuals).

Like giving up smoking though, staying away can be easier said than done. The forums and chatrooms can be addictive. We're social animals and we crave the company of others (level three of Maslow's hierarchy). Most of us trade alone at home, so it's natural that we seek out companionship in our work. Natural, but destructive. If you find it too difficult to switch off the forums, or close Twitter, then you're in luck. There's an app for that! There are web browser plugins and apps you can install that will block access to certain sites for fixed periods of time. Set one up to block your problem sites during market hours, and you will be removing temptation. It's a bit like the smoker locking their cigarettes up in a safe. If they really really want them, there's a way. But by putting them out of reach at a time when the temptation is not there, it makes it that much harder to access them when it is. See the *Resources Page* for links to some examples of blocking apps.

When it comes to the temptation to test new strategies that you pick up outside of trading hours, that's tougher. Trying to improve on what you have is a virtue, but it shouldn't be allowed to interfere with what's already working. So if you want to try something new, I'd recommend doing so in a simulated environment. That can be paper trading, or a full-on simulator. Ideally you want to do this with recorded data that can be replayed in real-time outside of market hours. That gives you the chance to try out your new thing in close-to-real conditions, but still leaves you free to trade your regular strategy, which pays the bills.

That just leaves us with those seductive price moves that everyone seems to know about except us. The stellar spikes that beg to be traded, even though they don't in any way conform to anything on our trading plan.

The way to deal with those is the same way we deal with contrast bias. Keep a model trade catalogue and train yourself to use it before *every* entry. That simple action should be enough to remind you, before you pull the trigger on the off-plan trade, that you're about to do something really silly.

Combine this with the trade logging that we covered when dealing with illusory correlation, and you'll have no excuses for taking the dodgy entry. When you write down in your trade log:

```
DAX / Long 2 @ 9,847.12 / 10:16 — Because the
price is shooting up
```

the act of putting those words on the paper should jog your brain into seeing sense!

Ultimately, beating social proof is about forcing ourselves to ask the question, '*Why?*' We want to know why we are doing what we're about to do. Why are we adding a new pattern to our trading plan? Because everyone's doing it, or because we've tested it and we know through our own data that it will improve our bottom line? Why are we jumping into a trade that everyone in a chatroom is taking? Because it's part of our proven strategy and we know, through our own experience and results, that it has a good chance of success? Or is it just because that's what everyone else is doing? And why are we about to go long on this stock whose price is going through the roof? Keep asking yourself *why*, with the aid of the model trade library and the written trading journal, and you will force your conscious brain to examine the actions of the subconscious.

Scarcity

Scarcity is perhaps one of the easiest heuristics to understand. It doesn't take much stretching of the imagination to see why Bob would be very keen to catch the one and only rabbit he has seen all day.

Fast forward fifty thousand years and we see the same thing playing out every time the stores hold their sales, especially Black Friday. Huge queues gather and shoppers storm the doors the second they open, desperate to get the bargain of the year. Do all these people wake up on the same morning and find that their perfectly good television has broken overnight, and must be replaced immediately? Or is the pull of the deep discount, and the fact it is so limited, the real driving force behind this phenomenon?

Scarcity is used by marketing professionals the world over, such is its power. I suspect most of it is entirely false, created purely to drive custom. There's no shortage of genuine scarcity though, and it never fails to push up demand... and prices. The most expensive car ever sold was a 1962 Ferrari 250 GTO. It went for a little over $34 million, not including commission of another $4 million. There were only 36 of the cars ever made (39 including variants). Very rare, very expensive. Go to any city where housing stock is limited — London is currently a prime example — and you'll see house prices defying gravity, logic, and austerity measures.

Our inbuilt desire for the rare is a dangerous attribute for the trader, and particularly so for the day trader. We start our trading session filled with enthusiasm and perhaps more than a little hope that we will switch off the computer richer than when we powered it up. We're here to earn money, and by jove we're going to do everything we can to make that happen.

The issue arises when we encounter one of those slow days. The clock ticks ever onward, counting down the time remaining to earn our crust, and the charts march endlessly sideways. When something resembling a good trade comes along we jump on it with gusto, determined to make it work. We've already seen how contrast bias impairs our judgement in this situation, making us believe a shoddy chart is God's gift to the markets. Now add the scarcity heuristic into the mix and we have an explosive combination, with out account balance the certain victim.

The trade need not be a bad one for us to fall foul of scarcity, though. A perfectly formed setup can turn around and bite us when, starved of other opportunities, we try and run it beyond where it was ever destined to go as we seek to make up for lost ground.

Scarcity gives us tunnel vision. It bypasses our judgement and tramples over our common sense. It's a menace, but it also happens to be a powerful weapon that can improve our trading no end when put to good use. We'll find out how in the next section. For now, let's move on to another sneaky bias.

Ambiguity Effect

Imagine we're back in the pub again. After getting in a round of drinks, and maybe some snacks, I pull a couple of envelopes out of my pocket. I put them down on the table in front of you, and ask you to choose one. I tell you that the content of the envelopes is a gift for you, but you can only pick one envelope.

The left-hand envelope, I inform you, contains one hundred dollars.

"What about the right-hand one?" you ask, pointing.

"Good question," I say. "Here's the thing. I can't actually remember how much I put in there. But I know it contains either two hundred dollars, or one hundred dollars, or nothing at all. It's definitely one of those three amounts."

Which envelope do you choose?

There's no right or wrong answer to this thought experiment. Some people will take the certainty of the hundred dollars and run. Others, who are less risk averse, will calculate that they have a two in three chance of getting at least as much from the right-hand envelope, and possibly more.

If you chose the certainty of the left-hand envelope, then you have just experienced ambiguity bias, or our natural tendency to avoid choices where not all the facts are known.

This cognitive bias can seem fairly benign. Helpful, even. Being risk averse is rarely a bad thing. If Bob finds a new, unexplored cave, which could hide a good supply of food, he's less likely to venture in if the light cannot penetrate too deeply and he can't see what's lurking at the back. His natural fear of the unknown, his aversion to the possible hidden dangers, ensures he won't get eaten by the tiger snoring in the shadows. Of course, it also means he'll never discover the massive horde of fat and very lazy bunnies that live there either, but that won't stop him eating, or surviving (unless, perhaps, all the other bunnies in Bob's home town have gone; in times of desperation, our aversion to risk diminishes).

Benign this cognitive bias might be, but as traders, risk is an inherent part of our business. Really, risk *is* our business. The unknown is our bread and butter. We deal in probabilities, not certainties. We cannot let an ambiguous outcome prevent us from entering trades. Which means the ambiguity effect can become crippling if left unchecked.

Hack It!

When we look at a possible trade, we're weighing up the probability of profit. We balance the possible win against the maximum we can lose. We pile up the elements of the trade setup that are in our favour, and compare them to the list of unknown factors plus the known risks. If the weight of probability is on our side, if the trade meets the criteria for entry according to our plan, we should take it without hesitation. Any delay is our ambiguity bias whispering in our ear, *'Yes, but what if...'*

It's almost inevitable. A perfect trade setup is a rare thing indeed, uncommon enough that we could never hope to make a living by trading only perfection. Every trade has to be a judgement call, and ambiguity bias wants us to move the line of what's acceptable as close to perfection as possible.

Learning to ignore that voice is one of the core skills of a trader. The good news is that it gets easier with experience, but we all suffer from doubt from time to time.

The first thing to remember when dealing with ambiguity bias is that actually, the outcome of the trade is entirely irrelevant. Our job is to execute the trade to the very best of our ability. Whether it makes money or not is out of our control, so the unknown future is not something we need to be concerned with. There's absolutely nothing ambiguous in our real job. We follow our plan and either take action or don't. As long as we measure our success in terms of whether or not we took the correct action, we have nothing to fear from the unknown and unknowable result. Reminding ourselves of this through the use of affirmations (see *Apophenia*) is the first step in hacking ambiguity bias.

The second step — because let's face it, we all think about the money sometimes, and that's when the doubts stall our decisions — is to move the focus from the unknown to the known. Instead of looking at a chart, or a financial report, and thinking about all the unanswered questions, put the emphasis on the parts of the trade setup that do fulfil our criteria. For example, if I'm trading my ERBO pattern on a stock, rather than worry about whether or not the pattern is good enough, I'll tick off the things I know to be true. Is the trade in the same direction as the market sentiment? Check. Is the price contained within the moving average? Check. Is there sufficient momentum to carry the trade through? Check. And so on. Build up a list of positives, and take confidence from those.

If you find you cannot ignore the unknowns or imperfections in a trade setup no matter what, then the final trick is to grade those negatives. I suggest using a flag system.

Taking the ERBO example again, I might say that not having the price contained within the moving average is a yellow flag against the trade. It's not perfect, but neither is it a deal breaker. Another yellow flag could be the trade not being in the same direction as the overall market sentiment. In other words, if the futures are up, the sector is up, and the indices are up, but the trade is to the short side, I'd be going against the market. Again, not ideal, but if the setup is good enough, not a reason to abort the trade.

But if I combine two yellow flags, then I can say that there's too much overall risk.

For really big problems, like a lack of momentum on the time and sales screen in my ERBO example, I'll assign a red flag. One red flag is enough to stop me taking the trade.

Using flags simplifies the decision making process. It normalises the unknowns and the imperfections into an easily digestible format. It breaks down the decision, forcing us to evaluate what we have already determined to be important about the setup (via our trading plan), and ignore what's by the by. The go / no-go decision is reduced to a flag-counting exercise, but the assignment of those flags still leaves enough room for an interpretation of the trade that sets us apart from inflexible robots.

Anchoring

Remember my ill-fated house hunting trip, with the contrast bias-aware real estate agent who sneakily showed me the best house last? Well, that wasn't the only trick he had up his sleeve.

The first house we visited was, among its many failings, considerably over-priced. The area I was looking to move to was a new one to me, and although I had had a quick look in a few estate agent windows (this was before the days of on-line house selling I should add), I hadn't paid much attention to the prices in the area. I had given the agent a list of requirements (which he gleefully ignored in those early properties) and told him the upper limit of my budget. So it was rather a shock when he introduced me to the first wreck of a house at ten o'clock on that windy morning.

When we got to the fourth house, the one that in contrast to the others looked like a five-star hotel, I was blown away. My one and only reservation was that the price would make it inaccessible. I thought it would be over budget. So imagine my surprise when the agent told me that it was on the market for the same price as the first property we had seen that morning!

The rest, as they say, is history. But there was a valuable lesson to be learnt, as well as the one about contrast bias. By showing me an over-priced property first, the agent *anchored* its price in my mind. The price became a reference point, much like the property itself did. So as we visited subsequent potential dwellings, I was not just subconsciously comparing the properties with the first one, I was doing so with an expectation that their prices would be comparable with the first property.

Price anchoring occurs every time we encounter a new market or a new scenario in which we have no pre-existing reference point. Like a newly hatched duck who sees its mother for the first time and imprints on her, we see a price and fixate on it. The trouble is, just like the duckling doesn't know if the first thing it lays eyes on really is its mother, neither do we know if our first meeting with a price is a reasonable valuation. Plenty of ducks (and other animals) end up imprinting on zoo keepers or farmers. Stories of kittens imprinting on big butch dogs are a staple of the Sunday tabloids. Human beings fixate on numbers that are in no way related to the objects they associate them with.

There have been lots of studies done on the phenomenon of anchoring, and the more you read them, the more bizarre they get. Here's one example. Researchers took a collection of students who had no particular interest in, or experience of, wine. They showed them some bottles of plonk, and asked them to think about how much they would be willing to pay for each bottle in an auction. At the same time they were considering this question, the students were asked to write down the last two digits of their social security numbers. Those who wrote down higher numbers (80-99) valued the booze, on average, at double the price of those who wrote down low numbers (0-20). Obviously there's no correlation between part of a social security number (which is, essentially, just a random figure) and the value of a bottle of drink, but the brain abhors a vacuum. When asked to think about the value of something it has no prior knowledge of, it will actively seek out any available number and cling onto it, regardless of the relevance of that information. It doesn't care whether the number is correct, or even if it relates to the item being considered. As long as the number is presented in the same context as the question, the brain grabs hold of it and uses it as a basis for its valuation. When better information subsequently becomes available (for example, a catalogue price for the bottle of wine), the brain still hangs onto the first, erroneously acquired data point.

We feel the effects of price anchors all the time. When we first start driving, we have to start paying for petrol (gas). As we get older, the price of fuel goes up. But we rarely consider today's price in its historical context, or in relation to the value of the product, or taking into account the effect of inflation. Instead we compare it to our internal anchor (the price we first paid), and conclude that fuel prices are crazy.

Credit interest rates, sales tax rates, mortgage rates, exchange rates, salaries, the list goes on. As we encounter each of these numbers for the first time, they become anchored, stored away as baseline figures forever more. We subconsciously compare current rates with those anchors as we move through life, and we're often disappointed by the result.

Anchoring is another shortcut heuristic rooted in our need to make quick decisions that are good enough. We're bombarded with more information than we could ever hope to process, so our brain filters it for us. And it doesn't just apply to numbers, we anchor on everything new we encounter.

Zapping back fifty thousand years, Bob isn't, realistically, going to try hunting every species that lives within a day's walk of the cave. He's not going to perform a statistical analysis of which kind of animal provides the optimum protein content for the amount of effort required to trap and kill it. He and his family will die of starvation or exhaustion before he's filled in half of his spreadsheet (drawn in sand). Instead, Bob's first experience of hunting, which probably happened when his father first took him out to show him the ropes, imprinted itself on his brain. He saw a rabbit warren, knocked a bunny on the head, skinned it, cooked it, ate it, and was happy. The episode lodged itself in his memory as a baseline. Every subsequent hunt could be compared to that. In theory, as new information came along — perhaps one day Bob caught a hare, and it was bigger and juicer than his usual lunch — Bob should update his baseline. Hares are better value catches than rabbits. But we already know that we're very good (or bad, depending on your point of view) at filtering new information. Selective perception (like confirmation bias) discourages Bob from changing his view that bunnies are best. Only if Bob moved to an entirely new location, one where he had no idea about the local flora and fauna, would he have an opportunity to reset his baseline information about hunting.

Does anchoring affect us traders? You bet! Everything we do is based around price and value. We're constantly evaluating the price of our chosen instrument and trying to determine if it's going to go up or down. Anchors can get in the way of that. A lot.

When we see a trade setup starting to build, we anchor on that setup as we first see it. We ignore subsequent data that might otherwise put a dampener on our enthusiasm. Anchoring causes *optimism bias*!

We're ready to open a trade, but we miss the perfect entry. Because we anchored on the price we originally targeted, we don't subsequently jump in late, even if it would be perfectly valid to do so. We wait for the 'perfect' (anchored) price, which never comes.

We can also find ourselves anchoring on a target exit price. This is particularly dangerous because it can see us stay in a profitable trade for too long, when all the signs are telling us to get out. We're desperate to reach the price we decided we were going for.

When a trade turns bad, we use the entry price as an anchor and tell ourselves we'll get out when the price gets back there. Of course, on the rare occasions that happens, we hang on a bit longer, hoping for profit. After all, our optimism bias is pushing us to prove that the trade was a good'un all along.

A variation of the last problem is that we can also anchor on our stop loss price. For example, we set a mental stop of 5 pips on a forex trade. After entry, the price blasts through the stop before we get a chance to close out. Instead of getting out anyway and accepting the larger than anticipated loss, we wait for the price to come back to the original stop price. Anything else is deemed unacceptable.

Anchoring can have longer term effects on our trading too. For instance, we can anchor on a trade setup the first time we try it. It doesn't matter if the outcome of that initial trade is a profit or loss, it will colour our expectation of subsequent trades. A poor first experience backed up with a second losing trade might be all it takes for us to write off a setup as worthless. Similarly, a positive first trade, backed up with another one or two profitable trades can convince us that there are riches to be had from this new setup, even when it then loses every day for three weeks straight.

Hack It!

Anchoring is a tough nut to crack because as studies have proven, once an anchor is set it's almost impossible to change it. It's as if the human brain is storing value information on a recordable CD. Any time we encounter a price or valuation for the first time, it gets written to the CD by laser and cannot be overwritten. Presenting new prices doesn't work, they just get compared to the anchor price.

It's not *entirely* beyond us to change an anchor. It can be done by altering the context in which the price information is presented. For example, when I was looking to buy the house, I had already got a price anchor for *house prices*, but that was for house prices in the area where I lived. I was moving to a new area, so my brain created a new entry for *house prices* associated with that new place.

As traders though, we can't go around creating new contexts for an existing chart. Once we've entered our trade and set our price target and stop, we're in. There's no going back and re-writing history. The next chance we get to set a new anchor is the next trade, and ideally on a different chart.

The perfect solution to the anchoring problem would be to try and avoid price anchors altogether. By being aware of the phenomenon we can perhaps reduce the effect, but it's hard-coded into our brains so we'll never get rid of it entirely.

We can't change price anchors, and we can't avoid them. What's a trader to do?

The answer is to take control of the anchors we set ourselves. Forget about profit targets or maximum losses, stop worrying about best entry prices, or any other price-based number. In fact, ignore numbers altogether. We can't guarantee hitting any of them, even if a trade works exactly as we had predicted. Instead, we must learn to anchor on execution. Because (yes, I'm going to say it again), execution is everything!

How do we do that? The same way we're going to hack our way around hyperbolic discounting. We're going to get out the big guns and destroy our anchors by hijacking our reward system. More on that — you guessed it — later on.

It's A Team Effort

As you've surely noticed by now, the cognitive biases rarely work alone. They interact, meshing their effects to drive our behaviour down a certain route, and it's not always the one we need to be taking.

Remember the diner example, driving down the road and choosing on which side to stop? Social proof helped us make the choice over which diner to eat in (the one with all the cars parked outside), but contrast bias also kicked in. It blocked out the idea that there might be another diner, an even better one, further down the road. We compared only what was in front of us, just like Bob and his two rabbits. And once we stepped inside the diner, it didn't matter whether the place was a dive or not, confirmation bias filtered our perception of the joint and told us that we had made absolutely the right decision.

Here's another example. Say we're out shopping for a new widget. It's been a long day, and it feels like we've visited hundreds of shops. None of the widgets we've seen so far were quite what we wanted. Now we're on the edge of town, in the last shop, and it will be closing time soon. There are only two widgets left. In other words, widgets are scarce, which makes them even more desirable. Contrast bias kicks in, so now we're only comparing what's right in front of us, we forget about all the other widgets we saw earlier. We need a widget and have to make a decision. Guess what happens when another customer walks in and begins singing the praises of one of the two widgets? Social proof helps us make up our mind. When that customer looks like they might then take the last widget left on the shelf, irrational escalation joins the party. That's the widget we want, and we're going to make damn sure we get it!

With these biases joining forces, it might seem like we have no hope of ever making a decent, informed decision. But fear not, all is not lost. Though our cognitive biases are omni-present, we don't use all of them all of the time. They're constantly there trying to guide us, like the SatNav in the car. But just as we can choose to ignore the dulcet tones of the GPS, so we can choose to think for ourselves and override the biases. We can, and do, regularly make decisions without their help. The real problem is that we rarely, if ever, are aware of *when* a cognitive bias is behind our thinking. We can't trust ourselves not to lapse into auto-pilot and let these pre-programmed rules define our route. That's why, if we want to really excel as traders, we must take active steps to hack the biases and have them work *for* us, *all* the time.

So far we've looked at some very specific techniques that are aimed at overcoming individual biases (though because they so often work hand in hand, disrupting one will usually help with several). The hacks we've covered are the laser-targeted precision bombs with which we can destroy contrast bias, or wipe out optimism and confirmation bias. They home in on the cognitive bias level of the WHAM pyramid. In the final section we're going to get out the big bombs and go thermonuclear on the lower levels — fear and greed. But before we get there, we have another level of that pyramid to examine.

LEARNED BEHAVIOUR

Introduction

As if all of those cognitive biases weren't enough to deal with, we've still got the top layer of the WHAM pyramid to deal with: learned behaviour.

This particular set of problems is less about evolution and more to do with the emotional and mental baggage we have acquired on our rocky path through life. These challenges are about nurture, rather than nature.

But fear not, brave hacker, for we shall overcome! Just as we have techniques to hack our cognitive biases, so we can infiltrate these new enemies. We will disrupt their ranks from within, and break down their defences so we may trample over their dying bodies to victory.

Or at least we'll push them aside so we can win a few more points on our trades.

Gambler's Fallacy

We're back in the pub. (I don't have a drink problem, honest. It's just that the pub is such a handy location. And I'm on the sparkling mineral water, thanks.)

I reach into my apparently bottomless pocket, and this time I pull out an evenly weighted coin. I toss it in the air and let it fall to the table between us.

It comes up heads.

I grab the coin, give it a practised flick of the thumb, and we both watch it spin into the air, then drop back to the polished oak.

Heads again.

The third spin turns up heads. And the fourth, fifth, and sixth. In fact for ten flips in a row, my perfectly balanced coin lands heads up.

I pick the coin up and prepare to toss it one last time. "What are the odds of it turning up heads?" I ask you.

What do you think?

When I pose this question to my students, they usually say something like "Well it can't land heads side up forever. Sooner or later it's going to be tails, and after so many heads, there's got to be a higher chance of it being tails this time."

Sounds logical, doesn't it? Perhaps, but it's the wrong conclusion.

In fact the correct answer is that there is a 50:50 chance of the eleventh spin turning up heads.

If you answered like most of my students, then you are afflicted with *gambler's fallacy*. To believe that the next toss is more likely to be tails is to suggest that the coin has a memory, that it somehow remembers the previous ten tosses, which is clearly ridiculous. Each individual toss has exactly the same chance of turning up heads or tails. It's 50:50, every time.

Trading isn't gambling. Unlike tossing a coin, when we enter a trade we have a degree of control over the odds by picking good trade setups that are statistically proven to have a positive outcome over the long run. We can stack those odds in our favour. We can also limit our losses and run our profits to come out ahead. But that doesn't mean we don't get hit with this common error of judgement.

After suffering a run of losing trades, it's very easy to think, *'The next trade must be better. I can't keep losing forever!'* But why can't you? The market isn't going to reward you for your previous string of losses. It doesn't know about those losses. You might have a memory, but the market doesn't. Each and every trade performs on its own merit.

Gambler's fallacy is learned behaviour, but it is shaped by those all-powerful cognitive biases. In fact, it's a specific example of apophenia, which we looked at earlier. It seems logical to us that a given sequence of events cannot continue to play out the same way indefinitely because in the world around us, that very rarely happens.

As I write this, we're going through the driest summer for the last fifty years. We haven't seen rain in months. The grass in the yard is yellow and dusty. The plants are dying, and crops are failing. Every morning we wake up and look outside and see more sunshine and endless blue skies, and every morning we say, "It's going to have to rain sooner or later!"

And we're right. It will rain. But just because it didn't rain today, that doesn't change the chance of rain tomorrow. We're so used to seeing some form of precipitation at least every few weeks that we believe it must happen. And when the clouds do eventually come, confirmation bias will reinforce this learned idea.

MARKET FORCE

The funny thing about gambler's fallacy is that it is so pervasive, so common, that it actually affects most markets. I would even go as far as to say that it's a major driver of price action.

I said above that the market doesn't have memory, but that's not quite true. The market has no memory as far as your individual trades go, but because a market is nothing more than a collection of people making decisions, it is inevitable that it will manifest certain group behaviours.

Indeed we see this play out every day on the charts. It's the basis of trend and support and resistance. When, for example, a resistance line is broken, we'll often see the price blast through with huge force and momentum. The market as a whole has been watching that line get tested, and collectively it has been thinking, *'That resistance can't hold forever. Sooner or later it's got to break.'* When it does, the market feels it has been proved right and traders pile in, confident that probability is on their side and that the price will keep going up. Gambler's fallacy in the masses actually helps push the price through.

The Solution

Leaving aside the fact that gambler's fallacy is a driving force behind price movement, it is an unhealthy belief for us as individual traders, and we should make every effort to eliminate it. Fortunately we already know how, because we've already seen how to hack apophenia in general: education, and revision through affirmations.

The Knowledge Gap

My youngest daughter is two. She's at that amazing stage of life where her head is like a Dyson for information, sucking up incredible amounts of knowledge during every waking moment. She constantly surprises and delights us with new words and phrases, and half the time we have no idea where she heard them. (I suspect she has a secret nocturnal life, sneaking out of her bedroom in the wee hours and meeting up with other toddlers to compare notes. Mrs Walsh does not share this theory.)

We're programmed to seek out knowledge from the day we are born. In the first hours of life it's all about learning where the milk is. Later, it's about mobility. We discover how to shuffle around, crawl, and ultimately to walk. Then comes communication. Listening, understanding, talking, reading, and writing.

It doesn't stop there. We're sent to school for years and, if we so desire, onwards to college or university. Up to two decades of our lives can be spent in full time education, learning every single day.

When we begin working, we continue to learn more and more. Specialised knowledge, unique to our field of employment.

At the same time this is all going on, we're learning social skills too. How to interact with others, how to negotiate to get what we want (milk, attention, cookies, toys, gadgets, pay-rises), how to please people by helping or entertaining them, how to stay safe in dangerous environments.

It is entirely unsurprising therefore that when we try and accomplish something new in life and we don't get the result we desire, we frequently assume a lack of knowledge is the problem. More often than not, we're right.

The other day, Mrs Walsh decided to bake some cookies. Now Mrs W is an excellent cook, and I aspire to one day be able to rustle up meals of the same quality that she manages apparently effortlessly. Cookies, though, are not her strong point. Spotting a gap in her knowledge, she prised the iPad out of our daughter's hands and looked up a bunch of recipes, filling in the information she was missing. I am pleased to report that this endeavour was a success, and that the resulting cookies were delicious.

There is a point to this illustration of domestic bliss, and that is that our desire to plug the knowledge gap runs so deep, we don't even notice it. One of the first things we ever learnt was that we could learn more.

And that can be a problem, because sometimes our lack of results is not due to a gap in our knowledge at all.

Trading is one example of such a situation. Here's how most people go about learning to trade, myself included:

1) The decision is made. "I want to be a trader!" we cry with glee.

2) Information is sought (we have a huge knowledge gap, so of course we want to fill it). "I shall read some books! Take courses!" we exclaim. Motivation is high, and our thirst for information is strong. We devour everything we can find on the subject.

3) We try and apply our newly acquired knowledge. "I'm going to make some trades!" We've read a ton, and it sounds simple enough. What could possibly go wrong?

4) We lose money.

Perhaps step four doesn't always involve loss from the outset, but in the vast majority of cases, new traders don't immediately see the kinds of profits they were hoping for when they started out.

It's at this point that our lifelong experience kicks in. *'I must be missing something,'* we think to ourselves, and we try and plug the knowledge gap. We assume a vital piece of information has slipped by us. Did we skip a chapter? We go back and read more, learn more, study different books. Then we try again.

If we still don't get the results we want, we repeat the process. Perhaps, we ask ourselves, there's some secret that isn't shared in the textbooks. Perhaps we can only get this secret from other traders. We delve into forums and websites and chatrooms and seminars. We learn indicators and systems and strategies of ever increasing complexity.

Here's the thing: by step four, we almost certainly know enough already. A gap in knowledge is rarely the cause of failure to profit. Most people who have studied trading to the point of taking live trades, but who aren't making the kind of money they want, already have enough facts to turn things around. There's a critical mass of information required to succeed, and the majority of people who are trying have already reached that mass. Learning more than is necessary only serves to confuse them even further.

Here's a completely different analogy that I hope will illustrate the problem. Imagine that you needed to build a house. You learn that you must dig a foundation and fill it with concrete; that you'll then build some walls out of bricks, add a roof structure, and cover it in tiles. That's one way to build a house, although not the only way.

If you've never built a house before, the chances are your first effort might not be great. The foundations may not be level on the initial attempt. The brickwork might not be very straight or true, and the roof could end up a bit wonky. But your basic knowledge is sufficient to overcome these problems; more practice is all that's missing. Every course of bricks you lay will give you experience, and each one should get a bit better. What you *don't* need is to learn how to build timber-framed houses, or steel-and-glass construction methods, or how to build with straw bales, or how to put together a skyscraper. There's nothing wrong with any of those techniques, and knowing them isn't a problem in itself. But if you're starting out, and you're trying to get a roof over your head, adding those different methods will only serve to confuse your own build. The added knowledge is superfluous. You may conceivably start mixing techniques, creating a building that's unsafe for habitation.

So what does this all mean for us as traders? It means that if we are trading, and are not making the profits we want, we must take a step back and look at the knowledge we already have. We should not automatically assume that there's a gap in that knowledge. All we need to know to make good consistent profit is what to trade, when to enter, and when to exit. If we have a basic strategy that covers those three things, then we already have all the knowledge that's required. Anything over and above that is unnecessary added complication.

I just want to reiterate that knowledge is a Good Thing. I'm not saying don't keep learning. What I am saying is that a gap in knowledge isn't always the reason for not getting results. In trading, it's rarely the reason. A gap in *experience* is more often the culprit.

Over Trading

Trading is a job, and like any serious endeavour it requires focus, attention, and discipline. When discipline breaks down, due to boredom for example, problems occur. One of the most common of these is over trading.

Over trading describes any scenario where the trader is entering trades that they should not be taking. It's possible to over trade with just one entry a day, just as it's possible to take a hundred trades in a day and not over trade. If the position should not have been entered, it is over trading.

Common instances of over trading include:

Entering a substandard trade, i.e. one that does not meet all the criteria on the trading plan.

Continuing to make trades after the maximum loss allowed by the trading plan has been reached, or the profit target for the day has been attained.

Trading too close to news or other events that, according to the trading plan, mean a blackout on entering new positions should be in place.

Trading outside of predefined times.

Trading setups which are not on the plan.

Taking positions that are not within acceptable risk/reward parameters.

These problems afflict most traders at some time in their career, but new traders are particularly at risk. A lack of experience, overconfidence in their ability, and a strong desire to get stuck in and make some money all combine to encourage the novice to jump in without due consideration. Sometimes these ill-thought-out trades will work out, more due to chance than judgement. When that happens, our old enemies *confirmation bias* and *illusory correlation* will fill the trader with erroneous ideas about what works, exacerbating the problem.

Easily the most common form of over trading is taking sub-standard trades or trading setups that are not on the trading plan. This behaviour usually stems from either boredom, fear of not finding a better trading opportunity, or greed for more profit than the market is offering us.

Whatever the cause, over trading is a disease that can empty our accounts and leave us for dead if not kept in check. Once we start over trading, it's all too easy to enter a spiral of doom, taking more and more trades like a desperate gambler piling chips onto the roulette table in a bid to win back their previous losses. An exaggeration? Not really. I've seen more traders fail due to over trading than for any other reason.

Hack It!

Having watched traders new and old make these kinds of mistakes time and again over many years, I have found that by far the most effective technique for combatting the problem is what I call the *Golden Ticket* method. It is as simple as it is potent.

Remember how *scarcity bias* gives us tunnel vision, and makes us take substandard trades on slow days? We're going to hack that very bias and use it for good instead of evil. Rather than letting scarcity bias creep up on us, impairing our judgement in slow-moving markets, we're going to introduce false scarcity before the market even opens. Don't worry, there is method to this madness.

My brother loves to play complex videos games on his state-of-the-art console. He zooms around exploring strange worlds, testing out bizarre objects and hidden rooms. At the start of each game he's pretty carefree; he'll jump on or into anything. Invariably this results in him getting "killed", repeatedly. When he gets down to his last life, his tactics change dramatically. Suddenly it's his final chance to beat his high score. One false move and he has to start over. So on his last life, he plays with caution, even a degree of thought.

Having one 'life' when trading has the same effect. It adds a degree of caution to our work. But hang on, trading doesn't have a concept of lives, does it? I'd argue our account balance is roughly equivalent, but we'll leave that aside. Instead, we're going to add the idea of lives to our trading day. We're going to create scarcity.

Here's how it works. For a given period of time, the trader sets themselves a hard limit of a single trade. That's it, just one trade. That trade is their Golden Ticket. Once it has been taken, once the ticket has been spent, the broker software is closed. It doesn't matter if the trade was a winner or loser, no more entries will be made until the next period of time. The Golden Ticket is a one-shot deal.

The period of time depends on the trading style. For a day trader, the period is one day. For a swing trader it might be a week. So in the case of the day trader, once they have made one single trade on Monday, they will close their order entry program and not make any more trades until Tuesday.

The reason the Golden Ticket works so well is because it forces us to really think about every aspect of a trade before pulling the trigger. When we know we only have one attempt at something, we will give it our very best effort. Because we've created scarcity right at the start of the day instead of letting it creep up on us, we're obliged to be on top form from the moment the market opens.

As we look at a chart setting up, we are beholden to ask ourselves, *'Is this really such a great pattern? Or is it actually quite mediocre and I'm just looking for action?'* We must examine every aspect of the chart with clarity of thought and purpose. Once in a trade, we feel compelled to manage it to the absolute best of our ability. We are spending our Golden Ticket for the day (or week), and we want to spend it wisely, getting the absolute maximum value from it.

Once the trade is over, we should close our order entry software to remove any temptation to have another shot. Charts can stay open, though. There's nothing wrong with paper trading the rest of the session, it's a good idea; it's an opportunity to gain experience without risk to our account. But we should commit to not taking another live trade until the next day, when our next Golden Ticket opportunity rolls around.

Naturally, we're not going to want to trade only once per day for the rest of our careers! When we believe we are ready, when we are making consistently good decisions and are managing our trades properly, that's the time to raise the limit to two trades a day. Now we have twice the potential to make a profit each day, but two shots is still enough of a limit to make us pause for thought before pushing that buy or sell button. How do we know when we're ready to raise the limit? By checking our results in our trading journal.

From then on, it's a case of rinse and repeat. Each time we feel we are ready to take the next step, we can increase our limit by another one trade a day (or week, etc.). Eventually we may feel we can remove the limit altogether, but actually I recommend keeping some form of restriction in place as part of the trading plan. It reminds us not to get trigger happy, to value every trade opportunity as golden.

The Golden Ticket method doesn't work only in one direction. We don't exclusively increase the number of trades we can take each day. When we hit a bad run (and we will, it is inevitable every now and then), it's a good idea to lower the trade limit. Maybe drop it to three, and if the problems persist, go right back to one trade a day. Making ourselves work for a raise will refocus our attention, and the restricted number of trades will limit our losses at the same time.

The Golden Ticket method borrows the concept of lives from the world of games. As it happens, games can offer us other brain hacks too. In fact, *gamification* is one of the biggest hacks we can implement. Gamification can subvert every level of the WHAM pyramid at once and take our execution to new heights, as we'll see in the next chapter.

ATTENTION!

Scientists argue about the average attention span of an adult. Lots of research has been done, and the results range from forty-five minutes at the top end, right down to just eight seconds at the lower end. Eight seconds, by the way, is a full second less than the attention span of a goldfish!

The disparity in these results is due to the different types of attention being measured. The eight second result comes from a study Microsoft carried out about the attention span of someone surfing the internet. The upper end of forty-five minutes comes from research looking at concentrated learning. Most experts, though, settle around the twenty minute mark as being our limit for focussing on a single task.

This is a big problem for us as traders, because even the most hardened scalper usually needs to spend more than twenty minutes in front of a chart on a given day. Long-term traders are at an advantage here, because they're taking positions based on research that can be broken up into bitesize chunks. For the rest of us, doomed to spend hours in front of a screen waiting for great setups to come along, solutions must be found to the issue of slipping attention.

When I first started trading I used to sit in front of a monitor all day, waiting for the good trades. The morning would be the easiest for me. I'd be refreshed, filled with coffee, and enthused about the new day and the opportunities it could bring. By around eleven o'clock though, I would feel my attention wandering. Unless I was busy managing at least a couple of frisky trades, boredom would sneak up on me. I'd start staring out of the window, day dreaming, or I'd open up my web browser and have a quick look at the news. (This was before Facebook and Twitter came along, two sites that have the power to suck hours out of the day!) Chatrooms and forums would tempt me. At least, I would tell myself, these sites were trading related. Talking to others wasn't bad, they were fellow traders, I might learn something.

By the time I finally got my focus back on the charts, sod's law meant I would have missed the best trade of the morning.

Afternoons were worse. After a hearty lunch my metabolism diverted energy to digesting food, which made it even harder to concentrate. I lost count of the number of times I dozed off in front of a screenful of stock charts.

Missing trades due to a lack of attention was only half the problem. When, by around three o'clock, my body naturally picked up some energy and I was able to refocus on the job in hand, I'd be keen to make up for lost ground. I'd start jumping into trades all over the place, entering almost anything that moved in a desperate bid to make up for lost time. The consequences, as you can imagine, were disastrous.

My case might have been extreme, but boredom is a real problem. That attention span is a limit that seems to be hardwired into the human brain. Remember, the brain hates hard work. Staying focussed on a single task is cognitively expensive. The grey matter will do whatever it can to slip back into a lazy dream-state, consuming as few calories as it can get away with. Any trader who needs to spend more than twenty minutes in front of a computer is going to face this problem.

Hack It!

Boredom attacks us on many fronts, so we need to build a series of defences, and even adopt some offensive procedures in order to defeat this particularly pernicious enemy.

Our easiest and biggest win comes from limiting the problem in the first place. The less time we sit in front of the screen, the less time we need to focus. Your scope for reducing your hours will depend largely on your trading strategy, but the benefit is so huge that it is worth considering changing your strategy if it means a possible reduction in the time spent staring at charts.

For me, one of the biggest changes to my own trading performance came when I moved to trading only in the mornings. I try now and have all my positions closed by about midday. I rarely open a position before ten in the morning. So instead of a full day fighting fatigue and boredom, the longest single period of time I spend in front of the screen is about two hours. And because those are morning hours, I'm working the way my body wants to work, concentrating hardest when I'm awake and fresh. You might work differently. Some people work better in the afternoon, or evening, or even the middle of the night. There are markets around the world, and forex trades twenty-four hours a day. If boredom or a short attention span is a problem, I highly recommend trying to make your trading strategy fit your body's natural rhythms, rather than the other way around.

CHUNKING

Next, try and fit some breaks into your trading time, whatever time of day or night you end up working. Obviously you have to be flexible with these. Clocking off to go and make a cup of coffee in the middle of a volatile trade is a bad idea. Having a three-minute break in a quiet time is a good one. Breaking up screen time between research and trading time is even better. This is what I do. Before the market opens I do my research and build my watch-list of stocks for the day. I break this task up into twenty-minute chunks, taking a short break between them. When I'm done, I have another break, usually a cup of coffee and ideally — weather permitting — a breath of fresh air. Then I sit down for those two hours of actual trading time, refreshed and raring to go.

You might have come across this idea of working in chunks of time. It's called the *pomodoro technique*, a name which comes from the Italian word for tomato. The original technique was developed by (Italian) Francesco Cirillo in the 1980s. Cirillo worked in twenty-five-minute blocks of time, with five-minute breaks between. He timed his chunks using a tomato-shaped kitchen timer, hence the name. He called one combination of working time plus a break a *pomodoro*. Typically a longer break is taken after four consecutive pomodoros. The method is a classic brain hack. It squeezes maximum efficiency out of the brain, giving the mind just enough break time to fulfil its need to wander from the task in hand.

A strict pomodoro method is obviously unsuitable for most day trading. We can't set a kitchen timer, then religiously get up and walk away from the desk when it goes off twenty or twenty-five minutes later. We might be in a trade, or about to enter one. But the principle behind the technique is sound, and it's the reason I do my pre-market work in twenty-minute lumps. Perhaps you can break up your day into manageable chunks, too?

BLOCKING

Now we've limited our working time, and we're breaking that up into smaller chunks wherever possible. However, distraction is rarely far away, so now we need to try and block out the temptation to do anything other than the task in hand.

Firstly, you should set up a dedicated working space for trading. If you have a room you can use for trading and only trading, so much the better. Similar to the way words program your brain when you use NLP, a dedicated working space can also program you to enter *work mode* when you are in it. If you trade in a place where you also relax, watch TV, play with your kids, or eat, then your mind will find it harder to make that switch.

Not everyone has the luxury of a single-use trading space. If that's you, then try and set aside a space where you will do all your trading, and where you won't be disturbed. The corner of a bedroom is good, but anywhere where you can close a door and not be interrupted is fine. The key thing is to always trade in that same place. The more you do so, the more your subconscious will switch automatically to focus-mode through association with the location.

If you have other people around you, make sure they understand that when you are in your trading space, you are not to be disturbed. That doesn't just mean no interruptions, it means keeping down the noise in the house. You are at work, and should be treated that way.

Finally, remove as many non-human distractions from around you as you can. Turn off the TV and radio. Get rid of games consoles, leave the mobile phone or iPad outside the room. Get the number of devices vying for your attention as close to one (your trading computer) as you physically can.

Your trading computer is your primary tool during trading hours, but it can also be the biggest distraction. Facebook, Twitter, the chatrooms and forums, they are all just a click away. You cannot cut off your internet connection if you want to trade, but you can put all of those tempting websites out of reach. There are lots of tools you can install on your computer to do this. You can configure them to prevent access to certain websites or services between set hours. So you can, for example, stop your computer from accessing anything except your broker, chart feed, and financial news site during market hours, thus ensuring you cannot sneak off to a chat room even if you want to. There are suitable apps for Macs, Windows, Android, and iOS devices. See the *Resources Page* for links to some examples.

Get Physical

A study from the University of Grenada has demonstrated what dog walkers, hikers, and gym members (the type who actually go) have known for centuries: physical activity leads to longer attention spans. Moving about gets the heart pumping and oxygen into the bloodstream and to the brain. Devices like FitBits and Apple Watches are catching on to the benefits of physical activity, reminding their wearers to stand up from time to time. You don't need an expensive device to remind you to move around a bit though. A kitchen timer is perfectly adequate. After all, it was just such a cheap device that sparked the whole pomodoro movement. Whether you use a clockwork timer, or a smartphone app, or you just count the passage of bars on your chart, make a point of standing up every ten or fifteen minutes. Waggle your arms about, jump up and down, stand on one leg; do whatever it takes to shift your heart rate up a few beats per minute. You'll feel better for it.

Better still, use a standing desk. There's fancy furniture on the market designed for working upright rather than slumped in a chair, but honestly you probably don't need it. My first standing desk comprised my regular desk propped up on a few bricks and breeze blocks. Not only did it cost me nothing, it had the added benefit of being "trendy" and "urban" (according to some of my younger friends!) When forced to stand for long periods, you'll naturally shift your weight around. You physically cannot nod off. Your body is primed for action, and that keeps you alert which means you can more easily stay focussed. Getting physical is brain hacking through whole-body hacking!

Drink

According to a study by the University of Connecticut's Human Performance Laboratory, dehydration can negatively affect energy levels, ability to concentrate, short term memory, and even mood. Mild dehydration is defined as an approximately 1.5% loss in the body's normal water volume, which is to say, not much at all. Therefore we need to make a point of drinking regularly, and drinking the right stuff. Alcohol is out for (hopefully) obvious reasons. Water is best, because the body can absorb it easily.

Make a point of drinking regularly throughout your trading session. Don't wait until you feel thirsty, because by then it's already too late. The laboratory's research showed that thirst doesn't really kick in until we are 1% - 2% dehydrated. So although you might think you're not dehydrated, in fact by the time you are thirsty, your mental performance has already degraded.

Music

I hesitated to add music here because it can so easily slip from being an aid to becoming part of the problem; music can be a major source of distraction. Generally speaking, silence is golden. However, used sensibly there is no doubt that music *can* aid focus. Some basic rules should be observed to get the best effect from music:

Absolutely nothing with lyrics should be considered, with the possible exception of made-up words, or lyrics in a language you do not speak. The human brain is wired for language and will latch on to any kind of verbal communication, sung or spoken. It just can't help itself. It will spend time and energy processing those words, and that's attention that should be directed at the job in hand. Lyrics are too much of a distraction. Instrumental music is the way to go.

No ads, for the same reason. Commercial radio stations are generally a bad idea because your concentration will be broken at the worst possible moment when some voiceover artist starts bellowing about the merits of a new washing powder. Stick to recorded music, or commercial-free stations. Spotify and similar services have more music than you can listen to in a lifetime.

Classical music is best for concentration. That's not just my opinion, there are swathes of studies that back up the claim.

Try and use the same music each time you trade. You'll get the same associative effect as from your NLP affirmations and from working in the same place every day. Your brain will become entrained by the music. Listening to the same playlist will bring your brain back to the same state it was in last time it heard it.

I've worked with a number of traders who swear by the use of video game soundtracks. This type of music has a couple of things going for it. 1) The tracks are carefully designed to bring about a focussed state of mind. Their purpose is to keep the player engaged in the game, hiding the passage of time. 2) Because of that, they go on for *ages*! Game soundtracks can be found for free on YouTube — just search for video game music playlist and you'll have enough to keep your ears busy for the rest of your trading life.

My personal preference for trading music is to use movie soundtracks, as they rarely have lyrics, they last about an hour, and they tend to cross a range of emotions which keeps the brain engaged without becoming a distraction.

Pay attention to tempo. Music is a powerful brain hack. It's like a direct line into our emotions. Upbeat music can make us feel good, and infuse us with energy. Whilst that might sound like a good thing for those moments when we're flagging (just after lunch, for example) it can also instil in us a false sense of confidence. Overconfidence often ends up costing traders dearly and is to be avoided. By the same token, we don't want to listen to something that will send us into a deep depression, or to sleep. A balance must be found.

Music is definitely worth experimenting with, but the golden rule is to never let it become distracting. Think of it as a condiment, never the main course. If you find yourself humming along, or anticipating the next track or riff or chorus, then switch it off and bring your full focus back to your trading.

Binaural & Monaural Beats

Your brain operates at different speeds throughout the day as it performs different tasks. That is to say that the electrical activity of your brainwaves can be fast or slow. When you are asleep, brain activity is low and the frequency of brainwaves is slow — below seven hertz (seven cycles per second). During normal day to day activities, it speeds up to anywhere from fifteen to thirty hertz. When you find yourself chatting with a friend while cooking a complex dinner, trying to stop the cat from stealing the ingredients, all while watching the TV with one eye, your brainwave frequency shoots up to over thirty hertz as your brain juggles all those tasks.

For deep focus and concentration, the optimal brainwave frequency is moderately slow — around ten to twelve cycles a second. It's the frequency band you are operating in when you first wake up, or shortly before you go to sleep. You slip into that band when you are doing an easy repetitive task, like washing up or ironing clothes. When you day dream, when you find yourself having great ideas or suddenly thinking of solutions to problems, you are in that magical ten to twelve hertz band. When you are trading, or doing other work, and you find yourself in the zone, with extraordinary focus and clarity of thought, your brainwave frequency will be around ten to twelve hertz.

Imagine if you could switch your brain to that particular frequency at will, as easily as you can switch a radio to your preferred station. You could sit down at your trading computer and immediately be in the zone, operating at your peak performance. This is the idea behind binaural beats.

Binaural (and monaural) beats are audio tracks that — through fancy engineering of frequencies and tones — entrain your brainwave frequency to that which is desired.

They're usually packaged as CDs, MP3 downloads, or software apps that run on smartphones, and are often sold as concentration or self-hypnosis aids. Generally they will be embedded in a carrier track, something that hides the relatively unpleasant tone of the beats themselves. That could be a piece of music, but is equally likely to be a noise track such as the sound of crashing waves, or heavy rain, or birdsong.

Some people say these types of audio aids are a load of rubbish and will cite a lack of sufficient scientific evidence that they work. Personally, I've have some great success using this kind of thing, and I know many of my students feel the same way. There is no shortage of free samplers you can download, cheap smartphone apps, and of course, YouTube has several lifetimes' worth of audio entrainment for free, including tracks that last up to three hours. So really, there's no reason not to try them out and see if they work for you.

MORE BRAIN HACKS

Hacking The Reward System

We saw earlier how fear is the engine that drives our decisions, even if we're not always aware of it. It operates at every level of Maslow's hierarchy, and in every aspect of our lives, including our trading. At the very top, we fear a loss of self-esteem if our results are not what we think they should be. We are afraid of being rejected socially because we're not profitable and so lose all the things money can buy that make us accepted by society. Working down the hierarchy we worry about a loss of safety, and ultimately an inability to meet our physiological needs, for the same reason. No cash, no food or shelter.

All of these concerns come back to our fear that we cannot attain the reward we desire — money. Of course, those fears apply to everyone, no matter what their line of work might be. For traders though, they are doubly problematic, and for two reasons. Firstly, because we can never guarantee the reward will follow our work, even if we do everything correctly. Periods of drawdown are a part of the game. We can trade brilliantly, and still lose cash because the market just doesn't want to play ball. Provided we stick with it, and provided our strategy has a positive expectancy, then we'll be fine in the long run, but that doesn't keep the fear at bay when the money isn't rolling in to pay the bills.

Secondly, and this is the real killer, that very fear itself messes with our minds and can prevent us from trading correctly. Our trepidation about a trade not working out can so easily make us hesitate before pulling the trigger. We miss the entry, or make a bad decision, and as a result lose money (directly, or through lost opportunity). That loss fuels our fear, and we are in real danger of entering a death-spiral. Apprehension causes loss which adds to apprehension which causes more loss. You only need to go around this loop a few times before you start to question if this trading lark is such a good idea. No wonder the vast majority of traders give up before they ever become consistently profitable!

So let's back up a second. If we analyse it, the entry point to this vicious circle of fear, the bit that sets us apart from those pursuing other careers, is that we can perform our job to an excellent level, do everything absolutely correctly, and still lose money. Our income does not have a direct relationship with our ability to perform our job. There are very few professions where that's so clearly the case. A good mechanic can find and fix a fault in an engine. Even if a car is found to be beyond repair, the mechanic will still get paid for having made that diagnosis. A good computer programmer can make a computer do anything their customer or employer wants. Bugs will inevitably be found, but they will be fixed and (punitive contracts aside) will not prevent the programmer from getting paid. A farmer is the closest comparison to a trader that I can think of. A farmer can tend a field throughout the year, only to have disease or bad weather wipe out all their hard work. It's no surprise that depression is rife in agriculture, and that so few new farmers are coming into that industry.

We like certainty. We like to know that we will be rewarded for our efforts. Trading is an uncertain game, and unlike farming, it doesn't take a year to enter the vicious circle of doom. Just a few trades is enough to make us start to doubt ourselves, and it's all downhill from there.

What if we could change that? What if we could take away the uncertainty? What if unprofitable trades didn't matter to us in the least? What if, instead of causing us to doubt our self-worth, a losing trade made us whoop with joy and slap ourselves on the back for a job well done? Provided that the job *was* well done, wouldn't that be a better way to work?

If we could disconnect our trading performance from the end result (profit or loss), then instead of our fear holding us back from taking trades, instead of it being an entry into the death-spiral, we could use it to drive ourselves forwards. Fear would go from being our biggest enemy to our greatest asset at a stroke.

This is what *gamification* is all about. We're going to hack our reward system and remove the *reward* of profit from the equation. We can't control how much money we get at the end of a trade, or even if we get any at all. So we're going to change the reward to something within our own control. We're going to turn trading into a game.

Before you turn the page in disgust, hear me out. Yes, I know trading is a serious endeavour, and I am deadly serious about helping you become a better trader. The fact is, gamification — reward system hacking — works. Everyone loves to win. So we turn trading into a game and make the aim of the game to *win* instead of to *profit*. We set up the rules of the game in such a way that *winning* is a result of executing our trades to the very best of our ability. We know that success in trading comes from execution, regardless of whether it turns a profit or not. Over the long term (with the usual caveat of having a proven strategy), we will make money as long as we execute well. Gamification keeps us executing long enough and well enough for that to happen.

There are psychological and physiological reasons why gamification is so potent. We're programmed to win. We want to beat others to the prize. Just look back at the cognitive biases and you'll see that they're all about winning. Social proof is basically a cheat-heuristic. We assume others are closer to the prize than us, so we go after them, using their apparent knowledge as a short-cut. Irrational escalation is us trying to do whatever it takes to win. The list goes on. Winning is in our DNA.

Gamification is so successful, we find it everywhere, and it starts before we can even say the word.

My youngest daughter encountered her first reward system hack shortly after she turned two. It came in the form of a star chart. Mrs W and I were trying to persuade her of the benefits of using a potty rather than a diaper, a trial that parents everywhere are familiar with. And like parents everywhere, we made the whole thing a game. When she used the potty, she got a star to stick on a chart. The growing lines of stars provided her the incentive and encouragement to keep going in the face of inevitable messy accidents and incidents.

The older children get *house points* at school, awarded for good behaviour or excellent work. Points can be deducted too, hacking the reward system from both ends. At the end of term, the house with the most points wins. Never mind the educational benefits and long-term prospects of doing their homework, that stuff is all lost on them; the kids are all about getting those points.

Supermarkets are well versed in reward system hacks. Who hasn't got at least one loyalty card? We love collecting up those points, almost regardless of what the end gift might be. I remember back in the eighties or early nineties, service stations in the UK all started giving away drinks glasses if you bought enough petrol (gas). Everyone I knew had cupboards full of wine glasses, more than they could ever use. And still they went back for more, because it felt like winning when the pump dispensed enough fuel to qualify for another set.

Prisons hack the reward system in the same way as parents, offering perks and time off for good behaviour.

Last year, Apple introduced a new product which hacks the reward system in an effort to make people get more exercise. The Apple Watch draws little circles on its screen, and they fill up slowly the more you stand or exert yourself. It sounds ridiculous to think that people who previously never cared about their general fitness would take action to fill in little digital circles, yet the internet is awash with stories of folks doing exactly that. Independent surveys of Watch owners have shown that it's not just a vocal minority, either. The majority of those questioned said that those circles had caused them to take more exercise of some form or another, even if it's just standing up more often.

This last example highlights the truly amazing thing about gamification: it doesn't really matter what the reward is, it just matters that there *is* a reward, and that it is attainable. Indeed the reward can have absolutely no real value whatsoever. It makes no logical sense, for example, that someone who is not interested in fitness would change their behaviour — in some cases quite radically — just to make sure they switched the shade of some pixels on a tiny screen. Isn't being healthy a bigger reward than meaningless circles? It should be, but those circles provide instant gratification. Getting fit takes time. More time than most people are willing to give. Filling in circles can be done in a day, or even an hour.

That instant gratification gets to the heart of gamification. It's at the core of why the reward system is such a powerful motivator.

The reward system lives in a region of the brain called the nucleus accumbens. When we experience something rewarding, the brain releases a neurotransmitter called dopamine into this area, stimulating the nerve cells. We feel that stimulation as pleasure. It doesn't matter what the reward is, the physiological effect is the same — a dopamine hit and pleasure response. Rewards make us feel good.

Drugs like nicotine and alcohol, all the way to cocaine and heroin, are chemical brain hacks. They physically stimulate the reward centre, causing massive releases of dopamine for intense hits, or highs. Such drugs are incredibly addictive because once our brain gets a dopamine hit, it wants another, and another.

It's this addiction mechanism that makes reward system hacking so devastatingly powerful. Something as simple as filling in Watch circles by standing up, or peeing in a pot and getting a star, has the same sort of effect on the brain as a heroin hit! And that means that the brain will go to the same lengths to get another hit via the same means. The great news is that gold stars and circles are easier, healthier, cheaper, and less of a scourge on society than drugs. It's all win.

Let's bring it back to trading. Our goal is to perfect our trade execution knowing that if we do so, profit is inevitable. We need to connect up our reward system to our ability to execute. We will give ourselves a dopamine hit for something within our control (executing a trade well), rather than something that isn't (making a profit). To do that, we move the reward from being the delayed gratification of profit at some unknown time in the future, to something we get right now. The actual reward can be virtually anything, because it's purely symbolic. The real reward is the chemical reaction inside our head.

Here are some ideas for symbolic rewards we can use:

Magic triangles. Set aside a page of your trading log. When you execute a trade correctly, mark a dot near the top left of the page. The next trade you execute correctly, mark another dot below it and to the left. The third dot goes below and to the right of the first. Now you have three dots, connect them up with lines and you've 'won' a triangle. Congratulations! Okay, I'll admit it, this is basically a star chart. But we're not two-years-old, so we can draw our own shapes.

Circles. It works for Apple Watch users, it can work for us too. And the best thing? We don't need to spend $350 or more to get started. A blank page in our trading log is enough to get going. Draw concentric circles for well-executed trades.

Food and drink. If you're not worried about the dietary effects, sweet or savoury treats make good rewards. It works for training dogs, why not traders? A better way to use food though, is in conjunction with circles or triangles. When you complete a triangle, or when your circles look like an archery target, have some chocolate. Or make it three triangles to get the reward. You decide, you make your own rules. All that matters is that you are consistent, and you don't take your reward before you earn it.

Now as any drug addict knows, the brain gets used to those dopamine hits, and over time it needs more to get the same effect. That's good; that craving for a hit is what will keep us executing to the best of our ability. To bump the effect though, we can inject a bigger hit every now and then. As suggested above, an edible treat for a certain number of points can be one such hit. We can think bigger though. Is there a movie you really want to see? Make yourself work for it — set it as your end-of-the-week prize. If you reach a minimum number of triangles or circles by Friday, award yourself that movie ticket. If you reach your goal before the end of the week, do like successful Kickstarter projects and set yourself stretch goals — bigger prizes for going above and beyond. Again, you make the rules.

The goals you set yourself must be attainable. If you never get to reach them, you'll never get the reward response you're looking for and you'll be no better off. At the same time, you need to make sure they're not too easy to hit either. There's no point making triangles just for *entering* trades, for example. All that will do is encourage over trading, and you'll lower your overall performance. Set yourself some criteria for what constitutes a *good* trade, and stick by them. If you remember back to when we talked about hacking the correlation engine with a trading log, one of the attributes I suggested logging was an execution score. This score is the perfect hook on which to hang the gamification of your trading. If your execution is terrible, if you hesitate all the time, if you take entries that are off-plan, or you stay in too long, running losers or overrunning winners, then you'll probably want to set your goals at a modest level. Award yourself a dot for your triangle when you execute a trade worth three out of five. When you're consistently executing at that level, bump the requirement up to four out of five. Needless to say, your goal is to be scoring five out of five for executing consistently, and awarding yourself dots, triangles, circles, stars, or chocolate cookies only when you hit those lofty heights.

It can be very tempting to also reward yourself for a particularly profitable trade, especially towards the end of the week. It's easy to think *'I've earned it,'* when you see a healthy bottom line in your account. Never give in to that temptation! From today forwards, profit is nothing more than a by-product of your execution. The only thing you should reward yourself for is excellence in following your trading plan. By all means knock yourself out and take yourself on a tour of the world if, at the end of the week, you've scored maximum execution points for every trade opportunity that came your way (not taking a trade you should have done scores 0/5, obviously). You deserve it. Just don't associate the vacation with the money you made.

Gamification is the single most effective brain hack I know of for improving trader performance. It might sound a little crazy, but it works like gangbusters. Getting started is as simple as setting your criteria for winning points, and deciding how you'll record those points. Most people see results right from the first point or two that they award themselves. It really does work that well.

Magic Mentor

Most of us have experienced the kind of day where we start the morning full of good intentions but reach the evening strangely disappointed that we didn't achieve all we expected to. It happens to me a lot, usually on the weekend. I wake up and decide I am going to clean the house, cut the grass, wash the car, do some work, and bake a cake, all before lunchtime. Then the day slips by and before I know it, it's dark outside and Mrs W and I are settled down with a movie and our favourite beverage. The chores I was so sure I would accomplish have been forgotten about.

It happens to us all (it's not just me, right?), and most of the time it happens when we have no accountability. If nobody is standing over us making sure we get the car cleaned, it's too easy to keep putting it off in favour of something more interesting. If we have a spouse, or a housemate, or someone we respect asking us, "Did you clean the car yet?" then we become accountable, and the chances of the job getting done are dramatically increased.

Trading is the same. It's easy to start the trading session with the best intentions in the world. We've read our plan, reviewed our model chart patterns, we know what we're looking for, and we're going to sit patiently until it comes along and then trade it by the book. Unfortunately, those intentions can slip out of the window after some time sat watching sideways charts. We want action, we want to put some money in our accounts, or some points on our reward charts. Substandard patterns start looking more attractive. Maybe we take a peek at something we wouldn't normally trade — non-watch list stocks, or exotic currency pairs — to see if there's something interesting happening elsewhere. Or we switch the timeframe of the chart, *squinting* for patterns that simply aren't there. If we reach our maximum loss for the day, perhaps we elect to take *"just one more trade…"*

All this deviation from the trading plan is possible because nobody is watching our backs. There's nobody standing over us, ready to scold us if we do something we shouldn't. We aren't accountable to anyone but ourselves, and it's easy to cheat ourselves.

So what can be done? The best solution is not the easiest: get a mentor. If there is any possibility of getting someone to actually stand over you and make sure you follow your plan, then I heartily recommend doing so. They don't need to be a trader. A friend, family member, anyone with a working pair of eyes and a modicum of intelligence can fulfil the role. What is important is that you have briefed them on your plan. A ten-minute overview should be plenty. Tell them "I'm looking for this chart to make patterns like this or this. When I enter trades it will be for this size. I won't allow myself to lose more than X trades today, or more than Y points. If you see me do anything other than that, ask me to explain why."

Now you're accountable to your mentor. If you go off-plan, you are going to have to justify your actions. Of course, you may also have to explain yourself even as you are on plan, especially if your chosen mentor is the curious type, but that won't be a problem.

Realistically, for most of us it's just not going to be possible to find someone available and willing to watch us trade all the time. That's why I recommend using a *magic mentor* — a purely imaginary one.

You might be thinking that imaginary friends are only for kids, but you'd be wrong. In fact, imaginary mentors have been used by some of the most successful people in history. Napoleon Hill, the author of the famous *Think and Grow Rich* self-help book, talked at length in that very book about his invisible counsellors, a group of people from history who he found impressive and wished to imitate. The group included Edison, Darwin, Ford, and Napoleon. He chose them based on certain character traits he wished to acquire. Every evening he would hold an imaginary council meeting with these men, conjuring up images of them in his mind, and imagining himself talking to them. As time went on, the meetings in his head became more and more real. Instead of Hill simply imagining conversations, the men started to speak for themselves, offering words of wisdom and advice. In fact at one point they became so real to him that he stopped holding his meetings out of fear that he was going insane, although he later resumed (on the advice of one of his imaginary counsellors no less), and even expanded the group.

Hill is by no means the only person to employ imaginary aides, and the method has become mainstream. I'm not suggesting that you need a whole group of advisors, but the technique itself can be used very effectively as a replacement for a physical trading mentor, and if used properly can actually be even more powerful than using a friend or family member for the role.

In your mind's eye, you'll need to create an image of your magic mentor. You can make them look however you want. Female or male, young or old, a real person, a fictional character, or a new creation, it doesn't matter as long as you can imagine yourself having respect for them. Donald Duck is probably a bad choice, Gandalf or Dumbledore a better one. Your own personal hero better still.

In your imagination, you should imbue this mentor with great wisdom. By all means add in some trading knowledge too if it helps. The main thing is that to you, they are someone you respect and can feel accountable to. It's worth spending a bit of time on this. Take fifteen minutes when you can be alone and relaxed in a quiet place. Close your eyes and build your perfect mentor. The more detail you can add, the better. What are they wearing? What colour is their hair? Are they sitting or standing? How do they speak? Detail adds depth and will make your mentor seem more real. If you can bring up an image of your mentor in your mind as easily and clearly as you can a parent or spouse, then they can — and will — seem equally real to you.

Once you've got your mentor fully formed, you need to reinforce their image. Try and spend a few minutes each day picturing them in your head. Talk to them. You'll have to imagine their responses of course, but that's all part of the process. The more time you can spend getting to know your magic mentor, the more real they will become to you.

Now when you trade, you can have your mentor accompany you. Before you get started, close your eyes for a couple of minutes and bring your mentor centre stage in your mind. Brief them on your trading plan for the session ahead. Tell them how you plan to trade, the patterns you are looking for, the maximum loss you are going to take, and so on.

Finally, as you trade, give a running commentary to your mentor. Do this out loud, as if they were actually sat beside you. Yes, I really am asking you to talk to an imaginary friend! And with good reason. Doing so will help in two ways. Firstly, vocalising (the process of putting thoughts into spoken words) is one of the single best ways of organising those thoughts. When you're watching a chart in silence, all sorts of things will cross your mind. Speak those things out loud, and you are forced to bring order to them, to consider them individually, and even to justify them. It's one thing to have a fleeting idea that *'This chart looks pretty poor but maybe it's worth a punt'*, and quite another to say that aloud. Most of the time, doing so will be enough for you to see how silly some of those ideas are, and you will quickly dismiss them.

The second reason for vocalising to your mentor is more subtle. Speaking your thoughts to them will again help to reinforce their image in your mind. The stronger the image, the more you will feel accountable to them. When you take any trading action, be it entering or exiting a trade, or holding position (or lack of position), having to disclose that action to someone you respect will force you to justify it, to explain the reasons behind it. If you are about to enter a trade after having already reached your maximum loss for the day, you will hopefully feel guilty. The more real your mentor seems, the stronger the sense of guilt and the greater chance it has of getting through to you and preventing you from taking an action you know to be wrong.

I know that nine out of ten people who read this particular hack will dismiss it as kids' stuff, or as madness. But the one out of ten who actually tries it and sticks with it is the one who is going to go on and succeed in trading, whipping those other 90%. To be extraordinary in any endeavour takes an extraordinary effort. It requires you to step out of your comfort zone and try something different. Doing the same old thing just renders the same old results. The magic mentor is a hugely powerful tool, and so I urge you to try it.

MEDITATION

If there is one 'secret' to my success in trading, it has to be regular meditation. It is the ultimate brain hack, not just for trading, but for success in every area of life.

Contrary to popular myth, meditation is nothing spiritual or religious, it's just a way of relaxing the mind with the goal of slowing brainwave activity to that all-important frequency of around twelve hertz or lower. It sounds almost too simple, and in a way it is. Yet an awful lot of people go through life without ever properly relaxing. Stressful day jobs, noisy households, televisions, tablets and telephones constantly blaring out sound — it's little wonder why. We are bombarded with stimuli all day every day. It's becoming harder and harder to switch off from it. Most people I know think that they are relaxing when they settle down in front of the TV, or when they pull out a phone for a game of Angry Birds, or when they go out with friends. But that isn't true relaxation. In all of those cases the brain is still being force-fed information. It is being asked to focus on gameplay or to follow a storyline or make conversation. To be *truly* relaxed, all stimuli should be removed, leaving the mind free to roam. That's what meditation does.

Before we look at easy meditation techniques, I should explain why it is such a useful practice. After all, mental relaxation and manic financial markets are polar opposites. Regular relaxation is important for two reasons. Firstly, it reduces stress like nothing else can. Sure, there are other ways of dealing with stress. A good game of squash, a long walk, or blasting aliens on a video game are all touted as working, but these activities don't go deep. They help us to ignore stress, to forget about it for a short period, but they don't make it evaporate in the way regular meditation does. Diverting activities are nothing more than a Band Aid over the effects of stress. Meditation is a cure.

Meditate daily, even for just a short period of time, and you will feel less stressed all the time. That helps enormously when it comes to trading. A relaxed trader makes better decisions. Do you remember back to when I talked about maintaining attention and being *in the zone*? It's that feeling you get when you have an amazing level of focus and clarity of mind, when everything seems to just click into place and is easy. You get to have that feeling every day when you meditate regularly.

The second reason I recommend meditation is because it is the most powerful way to take control of yourself. All of the brain hacks we've looked at throughout this book will help you beat your cognitive biases, or use them for good rather than evil. But even the easiest of brain hacks require at least a little effort. There has to be a conscious decision to effect change. We're creatures of habit, and our habits cause inertia. Once we've overcome that initial resistance, it's easy to keep going, but the effort to make that first move can be the hardest part of the process. Meditation gives us a direct line to the subconscious mind. We can quite literally *reprogram* ourselves to make that first change, to take positive action and implement the other brain hacks; to become better traders. When we are in a truly relaxed mental state, our mind opens. Like opening up the hood of a car, we can use that opportunity to poke around inside and retune our controls. We can turn down the loss aversion and the various biases, and turn up the discipline and motivation.

I know a lot of people who read this will dismiss the idea of meditating. It sounds too new age, too unrelated to trading, or just too odd. Those people will likely fall into the majority of traders who fail. The fact is meditation is a tool used by professionals the world over, particularly sportsmen and women. Professional footballers, racing drivers, jockeys, swimmers, *all* athletes at the top of their game meditate daily. It's an accepted part of the job. Trading is like sport in many ways; there is a need and desire to win, and a strong fear of losing. Traders and sportsmen both have a small fixed window of opportunity to get their game on, to hit the mark, to perform. If the world's top sportsmen and women are all using meditation, you can bet that it's going to help us traders too.

There are lots of ways to meditate, and here I will share two simple methods with you. They are both very effective, and either one will serve you well.

Technique One

If you have never done any kind of meditation before, then I would suggest you start with this exercise. Once you have done this a few times, you can add in the second technique.

Start by finding a comfortable position. Sitting is good, lying down better. Be somewhere you won't be disturbed, and somewhere quiet. If possible, try and do this exercise in your dedicated trading space. Your subconscious mind will make an association between the relaxed state you are going to create, and the place you are in. Any time you return to that place, your mind will seek to recreate the relaxed state. In other words, without any additional effort on your part, meditating in your trading space will make you a more relaxed trader.

Close your eyes and count down slowly from twenty-five to one. As you count down each number, try and visualise it in your mind's eye. That is, try and picture the number in your imagination. Concentrate on each number, its shape, the outline of the figure. There is no right or wrong speed for doing this, just take your time. Don't rush, but don't take so long that your mind starts to wander between numbers.

Some people have trouble seeing numbers in their imagination. That's okay, you don't have to picture a high-definition display of a figure in perfect clarity. Some people's imagination works that way, but most trading students I've worked with tell me that they see fluffy, poorly defined images, or that they don't see the numbers at all, they feel their presence instead, or are somehow aware of them. Some people even hear them. It doesn't really matter how your imagination works, because the numbers aren't the important thing here. The numbers are purely a focal point. Concentrating on them means you are obliged to block out other thoughts.

When you've finished the countdown, empty your mind of the numbers and move your concentration so that you are focussing entirely on your feet. Put all your mental effort into feeling your feet. Feel them become heavier and heavier, as if they were made of lead. When you feel they cannot become any heavier, move your concentration to the bottom half of your legs. Imagine them becoming heavier and heavier.

Move slowly up your body, repeating the process. Your knees, thighs, hips, belly, chest, hands, arms, elbows, shoulders, neck, chin, face, right the way to the very top of your head. With each step, stay focussed on that part of your body until it becomes heavy. You might find that as you do this you lose the feeling in your body as you move up. This is good! If that happens it means you are entering a deep state of relaxation.

By the time you have finished concentrating on the top of your head, you should be deeply relaxed. You can bring yourself out of the meditation by counting slowing from one to ten. When you reach ten, open your eyes and say (out loud if possible): "I am wide awake, relaxed, and my mind is clear and focussed!" You will still be feeling pretty chilled out at this point, and it's a great feeling.

The whole exercise should take around thirty minutes if done thoroughly, although you won't know how long you've taken until you've finished, because you will lose all track of time during the process.

When you try the exercise, don't worry if you break your concentration, after all, it is just an exercise and you'll get better with practice. You'll find random thoughts enter your head, that you'll lose focus, that your mind will wander. That's okay too. When it happens, just acknowledge that fact, then bring your focus calmly back to the number, or part of your body, you were concentrating on. Don't tell yourself off or admonish yourself, that will bring you out of the relaxed state. Also, don't worry if you fall asleep the first time you do this — I did! If that happens, it's because your mind has been craving the calm that you are offering it. It's been starved of relaxation and is taking the opportunity to grab as much as possible. Again, with practice you'll slowly gain control. You'll be able to reach a deep state of calm without drifting too far into sleep.

I'd recommend that if you've never done meditation before, you try and do this exercise two or three times a week. You might want to do more as it can become quite addictive, but as it's pretty time consuming, technique number two is better for use every day. Once you've got the hang of it, this first technique is great to do once a week.

Technique Two

This second exercise is a quicker way of reaching a meditative state, and can be used for shorter periods. It's ideal for use as a five- or ten-minute relaxer before you start trading each day. Use it daily and you will feel in control of your actions like never before.

As with the previous exercise, you will need to find a comfortable position, away from noise and disturbance. Again, your trading space is ideal. The more you meditate there, the stronger the association will be between your relaxed, calm state of mind, and the place you are in.

Close your eyes, then bring your hands together so that the tips of all your fingers on one hand touch the tips of all your fingers on the other hand. Just the fingertips, the palms of your hands don't need to touch. You will keep your hands touching like this throughout the exercise, so you might want to rest the base of your hands on your belly or your legs depending on how you are lying down or sitting.

Now count down from fifty to one. Again, take the time to picture each number in your mind's eye as you go. Focus entirely on each number. Don't think about how much time to spend on this, just take the time that feels right.

When you reach one, you should be very relaxed indeed. If you've been doing the previous exercise, you may well find that you feel you're weightless and floating, that you've become detached from your body. That's an excellent sign and means you've reached a deep level of relaxation. Your brainwave frequency will be below seven hertz.

You can remain in the relaxed state for as long as you need. In the next section we'll look at a few things you can do while there. For your first few times though, you'll probably just want to come back out straight away. To do that, count from one to ten, then pull your hands apart and say: "I am wide awake, relaxed, and my mind is clear and focussed!"

After you have done this exercise three or four times, you can reduce the countdown so that instead of starting at fifty, you begin at forty. A few more days like that, and then you can count down from thirty. Eventually you should be able to reduce the countdown to just ten, as with practice you will be able to reach the relaxed meditative state more quickly and easily.

When you are at the stage whereby you can meditate with a countdown from ten to one, you can really make the most of the technique, almost any time and any place. With practice you'll be able to meditate even in noisy environments. Boring commutes, waiting in airport lounges or doctor's surgeries, all those dead times become opportunities to drop into a quick meditation. These short sessions can be used for all manner of things.

You may be wondering why I asked you to touch your fingertips together during the exercise. This is a very useful step to include because it's another associative trigger. Just like how meditating in the same place each time creates a connection between that place and the relaxed state of mind, so touching your fingers together every time you meditate will make a subconscious link between your relaxed state of mind and the physical action. The more often you repeat the exercise with your fingertips touching, the stronger the link will be. You can subsequently trigger that association at any time just by bringing the tips of your fingers together again. Your mind will relax almost immediately.

This is a handy way of calming yourself in times of stress. If you're about to enter a trade but are nervous about hitting the button because of natural loss aversion, touch the tips of your fingers together and you'll find that fear drain away. If you're in a winning trade and feel the urge to exit early, to take the profit and run, touch the tips of your fingers together and feel a flood of much needed confidence. And the really great thing is you can use the same technique any time, not just in trading. Getting stressed at a colleague or family member? Touch your fingers together and feel instantly calmer. Been the victim of road rage? Use your fingers and avert an ugly scene. Meditation is a brain hack for life!

NLP

These exercises are both designed to get you to a meditative state, and that alone will help you stay relaxed and focussed. But there is much more we can achieve. While in the relaxed state, there are all sorts of clever things we can do. As I already alluded to, reprogramming ourselves is one such action. It's basically self-hypnosis. Anything we tell ourselves whilst meditating will go directly into our subconscious — that part of the brain responsible for 90% of everything we do. So once in a meditation, we can use our time there to repeat some affirmations to ourselves.

We've already looked at affirmations for combatting apophenia and ambiguity bias, and we can certainly repeat those whilst meditating. They really only scratch the surface though. When we're meditating, we've got the hood open and can tinker with our psyche much more deeply. We can reprogram ourselves on a much more profound level, effecting greater changes within ourselves. There's almost no limit to what we can accomplish, with a couple of caveats.

The first is that you must believe in any affirmation you make. Telling yourself "I am always in control of my actions," or "I always follow my trading plan," or "I trade without fear or greed," is fine. They are good, positive attributes, and we can totally get behind them. Our subconscious minds will lap that stuff up. But something like "I am the greatest trader who ever lived," will, unless you already have an ego the size of the moon, probably get thrown out by your subconscious mind's bullshit filter! You have to believe the affirmation you are making is possible for it to have an effect.

The second caveat is that you should stick to the same wording each time you use an affirmation. Always using "I never think about money when trading," is good. Using "I never think about the dollars when I trade," one day, and then "I always think in terms of pips not prizes," the next is just going to confuse your subconscious.

With those caveats in mind, spend a few minutes to come up with two or three excellent affirmations you want to use and stick with them. By all means add to them or change them over time, but make sure you stick with them a while because the more you use them, the deeper into your mind they'll go, and the more a part of your personality they will become.

Meditation combined with NLP is truly powerful stuff, and again, top sportsmen use these kinds of techniques every day. If they are good enough for Olympic athletes, they are good enough for us.

Wrapping Up

We've covered a lot of ground in this book. We've delved into the mysteries of the mind and seen how tens of thousands of years of evolution have shaped and moulded us. We've discovered that 90% of what happens inside our grey matter happens without conscious thought, and that much of it — well intentioned as it might be — is working against us when we trade. And we've covered a whole host of techniques for turning that programming around and using it to help rather than hinder our efforts.

It can seem overwhelming at first. Trying to put into practice all of these changes in one go the next time you sit down in front of a chart will likely confound and confuse more than help. That's okay, trading isn't a race, and we don't need to implement all of this stuff in one go, no matter how tempting that might be.

So instead of cramming, take the hacks one at a time. Each one you implement will improve your performance.

There's no right or wrong place to start with the brain hacks, but naturally I have some suggestions. I would recommend that you take up the first meditation technique as soon as possible. It gives you the most bang for your buck, and the more you do it the better you will get. Plus it will make it considerably easier to get over that inertia that affects us all, and to take action on the other hacks.

Next, I would suggest implementing gamification. Hacking your reward system will improve your trade execution like nothing else, and like meditation, the sooner you start the sooner the effect can build.

With those two in place, you can then move on to the cognitive bias hacks. Take them in any order you like. If you keep a trading log (and you should) then you probably already know in which areas you need the most help. Attack your weaknesses accordingly, and watch your profits grow.

All of this assumes, of course, that you have a solid trading plan and a good, proven strategy with positive expectancy. Brain hacks make you a better trader; you owe it to yourself to have a plan to match your talents.

I wish you good trading!

Also by Harvey Walsh

Bitcoin is the new frontier of finance. Huge returns are possible, but with no shortage of scammers and hackers eager to get their hands on your profits, it's the 'Wild West' of the trading world. That's why in *Bitcoin For Traders*, as well as showing you how to trade the exciting new cryptocurrency markets for maximum returns, Harvey also teaches you how to stay safe.

How To Day Trade Stocks For Profit is a complete course designed to get you quickly making money from the stock market. No previous trading experience is necessary. Easy to read and jargon-free, it starts from the very basics, and builds to a remarkably simple but very powerful profit generating strategy.

Would you like to discover the forex trading strategies used by professional FX traders? In *How To Day Trade Forex For Profit* Harvey Walsh pulls back the curtain and invites you into the lucrative world of currency trading. Written in his trademark plain English, this jargon-free book takes you through everything you need to know in order to start trading the foreign exchange market.